T0273596

WARRIOR
MINDSET

WARRIOR MINDSET

How to leverage your leadership strengths
to achieve extraordinary results.

GERMAINE C. GASPARD

Clovercroft Publishing

Warrior Mindset: Leveraging Leadership Strengths

Published by Clovercroft Publishing, Franklin, Tennessee

Edited by Adept Content Solutions

Cover and Interior Design by Adept Content Solutions

Printed in the United States of America

978-1-948484-83-1

CONTENTS

What is your purpose?

The question of purpose is a question we are all ordered to answer at some point in our lives. Discovering it dramatically impacts our quality of life and the joy we experience while navigating life's ever-changing stages. Some people never discover it, finding themselves at the crossroads of indecision, feeling empty and wondering what their life was all about. Purpose is everything. We all have a distinct purpose in this world. During the process of being conceived, 1.2 billion potential humans were released to impregnate one opportunity to be born. Guess who made it: *you*. You are not one in a million. *You* are one in 1.2 billion. *You* are not an accident. *You* have a unique and distinct purpose. Once you know what your purpose is, in which ways do you move forward to fully experience and accomplish that purpose?

I wrote this book because I want to use my gifts of mentorship to assist you to live your life on purpose.

Your purpose is the source for the motivation that gets you *going* in the morning and keeps you *growing* throughout life. Your purpose is the fuel that empowers the gifts of discipline and focus. These gifts make space in our lives for the opportunity to *grow* through life instead of merely going through life and living a less-than-fruitful existence. Without growth and without purpose, we are just seeds of potential. Seeds are small and insignificant. Without the proper fertilization, seeds lie dormant and deposit their wealth into the cemetery through death. A seed requires dirt, water, and pressure. Like seeds, we all have a great destiny inside of us that can grow into a mighty tree and eventually an entire forest that will create an impact for generations.

We all desire the best for our loved ones, our children, our families, and ourselves, but in order for us to reach our highest potential, we have to have a warrior mindset. Life is not easy; growth requires the overcoming of odds and obstacles. We have to develop the ultimate skillsets of survivability and thrivability in all terrains of life. Our first survival experience is birth. During which our warrior code of survivability and thrivability is established. During birth we are intuitively awakened into a warrior consciousness that shapes our innate gifts. As all seeds we are submerged in water and darkness until we are pushed out of the environment we have outgrown. This experience is replicated hundreds of times in our life. Our lives are an everchanging cycle of being planted, and either developed in the dark and reborn through our growth into a new environment, or stagnated because our in ability to out grow our present situation.

While working as a team member inside the Texas Ranger Special Ops Division, my teammates and I conducted missions where surviving wasn't a sufficient answer. We had to thrive because people were depending on us. Mothers depended on us to bring their children home, our community depended on us to catch criminals. We depended on one another so that our sons and daughters would continue to have fathers. Likewise, the world is depending on you to give it the gift of your purpose.

This book will offer you a detailed, inside look into the warrior's mindset. My desire is for you to understand the meaning of being a warrior and to wage war on the things that destroy or defeat your dreams. There are all kinds of wars, both physical and nonphysical. The only constant about war is that it must be fought and won first in your mind and then in the realm in which the war is being waged.

What are you facing? What are you are battling? It may be anxiety, depression, a career choice, a relationship challenge, or the struggle to gain a financial foothold. No matter where you are now, I want to change the way you see a job, the way you see your work, and the way you approach opportunity in life, in business, and in your relationships.

My life changed the moment I decided to walk away from everything that required me to be a smaller version of myself than my purpose, dreams, and visions identified me to be. I even had to walk away from *me*. I had to walk away from toxic thinking. By selecting my thoughts rather than allowing them to be selected by default, I began to select my actions. I started walking away from the things that discounted my value and walking toward the things that added to my understanding of value. I changed my perspective by changing my environment and the environment of my thoughts. I walked away from TV, the radio, and all other means of inputs that touched any of my five senses. I guarded my five senses as though my life depended on it—I found that it did.

I exchanged news outlets for audio books selected by content that expanded my capacity. I exchanged radio stations that fed me ideas selected by others for songs filled with content that I wanted to learn. I even exchanged going to church publicly for personally selected messages to give me knowledge that lessened the degree of my ignorance. By worshiping in private, I was able to build an authentic relationship with my creator that stood on transparency. I had to be naked in private before I could be clothed in public.

This requires focus and discipline.

I've learned that discipline is being a disciple of something that is bigger than yourself. I have been a warrior all my life. Through paramilitary and police work, it has been my job to serve and protect. My chosen discipline in life has been to keep people safe and coach others how to be safe and grow into success. No matter their age, I help them understand the falsity of fear and the reality of danger. Warriors don't just go through the motions and wait for someone to strike. They are the hammers, not the nails, in their lives. They live life on purpose, mapping out their goals—the territory they want to conquer—and they create game plans on how to get there. They avoid the enemy or battle based on success-driven, not ego-driven, decisions.

When I began to focus and find my purpose, I was able to make decisions without hesitation because the decisions were as easy as measuring whether they took me to or from my purpose. I began to make sacrifices others couldn't understand and make moves with an almost prophetic ability. The original intent of my life began to make the decisions of my life for me, with me, and through me.

This mindset is applicable to life and business and to the enemies of your God-given purpose and calling—even when the enemy looks at you every time you stand in the mirror.

From birth, we are trained to do three things in our lives. Become employed, get married and have a family. This is most people's thought process, however, I have a different perspective. When you see a bird flying, is that bird not working? Better yet, working properly—working from the perspective of doing what it was designed to do? How obvious is it that a bird in flight is working properly? Likewise, we need to find our work and what life we were created to live. You can't be fired from *your* work—no different than a bird can't be fired from flying. However, you can be fired from a job. Rather than work at a job, we need to deploy ourselves into our societies for the betterment of mankind. We are the agents of greatness in this world. We are the seeds of potential that will create the future.

Each of us is different, just as our fingerprints are unique. Our purpose, like our fingerprint, is unique to our own personal life blueprints.

During this reading journey, you will realize this book is about you and about developing leadership in your life. True Leadership creates sustainable happiness in your life. It is impossible to be successful without happiness. The foundation of happiness is fulfillment. Gaining the world at the cost of losing your happiness is the tale told by many celebrities. When these celebrities are asked if they feel successful, the answer is often no. The true definition of success is measured by the fulfillment of purpose. Hopefully you'll learn that balance is more than a buzzword and requires focus and clarity in attaining what you want. You must develop the discipline to take the steps to achieve it. Happiness doesn't have to be situational, depending upon whether you have the right girlfriend, boyfriend, spouse, or dream job.

Happiness is sustainable.

Creating happiness in your life, in our youth, and in our leaders so that they can connect the dots of true fulfillment, success, and realized potential is key. As previously stated, it is impossible to truly be successful without happiness. Success and happiness are a couple that when divorced birth disappointment and unfulfillment. This book will help you discover ways to find your purpose and use emotion (energy in motion) and resources (filling from the source) to keep growing. Reading this book, will create an abundance of self discovery questions, that only you can answer. These answers will reappear as clear and as unique as your fingerprint in life.

What is my purpose?

What makes my heart sing?

What am I becoming?

What is the difference between doing and becoming?

What do I have to offer the universe?

How do I find the direction and the purpose?

Whatever you would do for free, that is where you start. That is where you find your purpose. **If you didn't have to worry about water, food, or shelter, and you could just do what you love, what would that be?**

Everything starts with you. I'm here to help you on this journey and to show you a few things that worked for me. I want to build something that ensures every child and adult can find a way to grow and discover their strength and purpose. As you grow, you will eventually outgrow the pot you presently reside in. This book will help give you the space to grow and be the best version of you possible. As you read through these chapters, take notes on the blank pages right inside the book! They are designed with you in mind. Feel free to ask yourself the important questions:

Who am I?

Where am I going?

What is the source of my power or faith?

Why am I here, and why am I doing this?

YES/NO
Describe

Detail

List

Confirm

YES/NO
Describe

Detail

List

Confirm

Is this ego driven or success driven? (Ego-driven decisions don't bring fulfillment.)

Am I doing this because I want this or because it is good for the whole?

Do the people in this circle add value to me or my dreams?

How do I add value to where I am going?

If I am not adding value, why am I going?

Why do these questions matter?

Things will get hard. That is a certainty. You can't answer your *why* until you know *what* you stand for. There are lots of things that we are willing to live for, but what you stand for is what you are willing to die for.

The death spoken of here, more often than not, is a non-physical death. Rarely do we find ourselves in situations where physical death is an option. More often we find ourselves in situations requiring us to define what in our life we are willing to sacrifice. **The question is simply what are you not willing to live without?**

This is the thing that's most meaningful to you.

Once we strip all the shine and luster, what are you not willing to give away or do without? This is where your stand lays.

We have seen, read, and heard countless stories of human triumph. In these inspirational stories, great men and woman lived through insurmountable pain, pressures, and odds. The ability to survive through extreme and horrible conditions is the product of the human spirit and its ability to be resilient. We know we can live *with* pain and adapt to live in horrendous situations. Therefore, living *with* something is not a testament to our core or what drives us to love. What *is* a testament to our core are the things hidden in those stories that the hero has refused to give away, such as their dignity, honor, beliefs, or integrity.

As children, my brothers and I went to the Boys Club during summer breaks from school. One day, my mother gave me a couple of dollars to buy my two brothers and I lunch at a McDonald's near the club. I was so excited about going to McDonald's, and I bragged how my brothers and I had money to go to McDonalds.

While changing clothes in a locker, I was confronted by three older boys. One of them said, "Give me the money!" I

YES/NO

Describe

Detail

List

Confirm

YES/NO
Describe

Detail

List

Confirm

responded, "What?" Another of the boys hit me and said, "Give us your McDonald's money!" I was scared, and the shot to my face hurt, but I didn't consider that. What I thought about was that if I gave away the money, then my brothers would be hungry all day and would have to go without eating.

I held on to the money and fought. I took several more licks and ended up pushed into a locker, but! I kept the money. My brothers and I walked to McDonald's that day, and we ate our lunch. I remember the pride I felt as they enjoyed the treat that our mother gave us. I never told them or my mother what happened, but I learned something that day about myself and life.

What allowed me to take the beating wasn't what I was willing to live with but rather a deep-seated core value that I had no idea existed inside of me. I wasn't willing to exchange my comfort for my brother's pain.

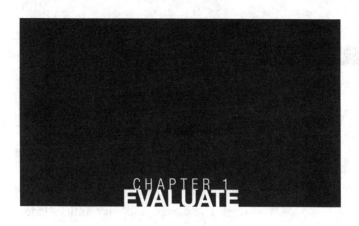

CHAPTER 1

EVALUATE

Where are you now?

Nothing in life can be achieved without understanding where you are in the moment. While working on a special operations team, we were tasked with acquiring an individual wanted for murder and assault of several peace officers. The suspect lived on a compound on a plot of wooded land that covered more than thirty acres. Once the suspect identified local agencies approaching, he fled into a forest of trees and disappeared into prefabricated hiding places

So how did we get him? We created a plan to insert as a team onto the property around 0300 (3:00 a.m.). We rucked (walked with 70 pounds of water, ammunition, supplies, and gear) and navigated

YES/NO
Describe

Detail

List

Confirm

YES/NO
Describe

Detail

List

Confirm

several miles through the dense forest without the use of any ambient light in the darkness of night, stealthily moving to a position just inside a tree line outside the target's home. Doing so required us to use a system that consistently established and confirmed our current locations to help us adjust to our desired location. We used compasses and waypoints (landmarks). Once inserted into the terrain, we identified where we stood and where the target (our purpose) was in relation to our location. We then established a waypoint based on the environment and our desired mission of staying stealthy and uncompromised. Once we established a waypoint, nothing else mattered other than getting to the waypoint. We continued the process until we met our original objective. Without a true understanding of where we stood, we never could have found our way to where we needed to be. In order to bridge the gap from where you are now to where you want to go in the future, you must have a clear understanding of where you are currently situated.

The only way to travel to where you want to be is to know where you are......

With regard to war and battle:

Out of every one hundred men, ten shouldn't be there, eighty are just targets, nine are the real fighters, and we are lucky to have them, for they make the battle. Ah, but the one, one is a warrior, and he will bring the others back. (Heraclitus, c. 500 BCE)

When reading this quote, we see the warrior. We see the warrior as he is during the fulfillment of his potential. We often fail to realize the warrior was once one of the ten, one of the ten who shouldn't even be there

What happens when you have lived your life on purpose and you've walked or even run down the wrong path? I say there is no wrong path. You were meant to be where you are right now. There will be moments when you've followed the enemy unwittingly or when you've allowed yourself to stay too long in a destructive relationship, or you've made decisions that aren't the best. Everyone has. But remember that every superhero has an origin story. Often, they're tragic and lead the superhero down a dark path before they discover that they're the hero we know them to be. Batman's legendary origin story is a powerful example.

As a young boy, he was simply Bruce Wayne until his parents came face to face with an armed robber in the night after leaving a movie theater. The thief fired his gun twice, killing both of Bruce's parents.

YES/NO
Describe

Detail

List

Confirm

There are moments in your life that will define you and make you who you are; who you're becoming and the decisions you make along the way sharpen your sword.

How sharp is your sword?

List three sharpening decisions you've made and three decisions that have dulled you. Compare the decisions. Which were ego driven, meaning they fed a personal desire, and which were success driven, meaning they fed your purpose?

Decisions		(please circle)
1. _____	sharpening decisions	ego- / success-driven
2. _____	sharpening decisions	ego- / success-driven
3. _____	sharpening decisions	ego- / success-driven
4. _____	dulled decisions	ego- / success-driven
5. _____	dulled decisions	ego- / success-driven
6. _____	dulled decisions	ego- / success-driven

YES / NO

Describe

Detail

List

Confirm

This tragic origin story was the catalyst for the journey to come and the creation of Batman himself. But that one incident didn't just create Batman in a moment. It was the journey he took after the adversity that connected the dots of self-discovery and allowed him to access the warrior within. Bruce dedicated his life to defeating criminals like the one who stole his childhood from him, and as a result, he traveled the globe studying how to become a warrior. Batman would not have become a hero had it not been for his origin story.

What's your catalyst?

The story doesn't have to be tragic, only defining.

Each of us will reach the forks in the road that await us. When I think of standing at the fork in the road, I'm reminded of a Jay-Z song. The lyrics in the song say, "I drove by the fork in the road and went straight." I love that verse because it identifies that forks in the road are merely identified routes, and you have the ability to color outside the lines.

What will you do?

How will you decide what path to take?

Will your decision be tied to principle and purpose?

YES/NO
Describe

Detail

List

Confirm

YES/NO

Describe

Detail

List

Confirm

No matter what your story is, the point is that there is no testimony without their first being a test. The process of being made is grueling. Our growth walks hand in hand with our failures. They are intertwined. They are intertwined, like cousins, lovers, friends, and foes.

Your life will change as mine did the moment you decide to be the author of your life's story and not a mere a character in it. Understand that someone else could win with the hand you've been dealt. For every job you received, someone else didn't and was blessed by the moment of failure. For every mistake you've made, someone made that very same mistake before you and learned or perhaps even benefited from the experience.

True warriors don't seek outside targets or objectives. They seek the fulfillment of purpose coded in their DNA/make-up. Therefore, all external objects are destroyed or sparred based on the mission of purpose rather than the need for the destruction of an external opponent.

Our lives are the result of perceptions: how we perceive ourselves, how we perceive others, and how we perceive the world around us. Once you identify that you were made by the creator for a purpose that only you can fulfill, you can begin your walk down the path of success and fulfillment.

Notes

_____

_____

_____

_____

_____

_____

_____

_____

_____

_____

_____

_____

_____

_____

_____

_____

_____

_____

_____

_____

_____

_____

_____

_____

_____

_____

_____

_____

_____

_____

_____

_____

_____

_____

_____

_____

_____

_____

_____

_____

_____

_____

_____

_____

_____

_____

CHAPTER 2
CORE VALUES

What are your core values? Show me someone without clarity of their core values, and I'll show you someone that's experimenting with life, living a life of trial and error without specific intentions, bumping and tripping along the path of life without direction. If you don't know what your core values are, you cannot answer the questions all humans seek to answer:

- **Who am I?** (the question of identity)

- **Where do I come from?** (the question of origin)

- **What can I do?** (the question of potential)

- **Why am I here?** (the question of purpose)

YES/NO
Describe

Detail

List

Confirm

9

YES/NO
Describe

Detail

List

Confirm

In 2014 I experienced the devastation of divorce. During that period, I had to make some major decisions. The most important decisions I had to make were the decisions that affected my children. Within the span of my marriage, I was given the gift of an awesome and amazing son. While settling terms of the divorce, I was faced with dealing with the attorney general's office. This was the first time I had ever experienced this. I quickly learned that neither they nor the courts cared about how good of a father I was. During the proceedings, I was faced with a decision: acceptance of an erroneous child support order declaring I was only going to see my son on Wednesdays and every other weekend, setting a monthly payment and evaluation of over one thousand dollars based on the visitation order, or continuing to spend money I didn't have on attorney fees and fighting for what was the true situation.

The true situation was that I had my son for three hours every morning as I prepared him for school five days a week, while also picking him up from school on Fridays and keeping him every week-end—in addition to coaching every team he was a part of. As I kept my son, I provided for whatever he needed and took him on vacations with me as we traveled.

Because I could answer the questions above, the answer and the sacrifices I made and make were easily made. I accepted the child support order and paid for the right to continue to be in my son's life to the degree we both needed for our best existence.

- **Who am I?** I am Father.

- **Where do I come from?** I come from a place absent of lack.

- **What can I do?** My potential is without limits.

- **Why am I here?** I build, reinforce, and rebirth Transformational Leaders and Champions.

The answers to these questions give an understanding of what to say yes to and, more importantly, what to say no to. If you haven't taken the time to define your values, begin to shape them as you read this book. I have several core values. Here are a few.

Balance: At its core, balance is understanding that there are both positive and negative energy. Life is about finding the balance and the midline of both these energies. In life, balance is understanding that you should always begin with

YES/NO
Describe

Detail

List

Confirm

YES/NO
Describe

Detail

List

Confirm

the end in mind. The energy we use to pull and push people, places, and things in our life should always be determined by our need to generate and produce a desired purpose. Balance is understanding both the push and pull of life. Balance sounds like a simple concept, but it isn't. It is complex because everyone's balance is different.

Endurance: At its simplest definition, endurance is how often you can exert an energy toward a goal consistently. It is how much you can push before you become exhausted and can't continue.

We all have a designated amount of energy granted to us. Our energy bank can grow, and our endurance can improve. Anything that we are outputting, we can make more sustainable. We live in time only because we haven't made it to eternity. As sons and daughters of the manufacturer, we first have to find our purpose. Then we can learn to use time as a resource for our purpose. Endurance is the vessel or the transport we use to navigate time. Endurance measures how well we use the resource of time.

Flexibility: Flexibility creates power. It is the ability to take our balance and endurance to the next level. None of us is stronger than natural law. Flexibility is what helps us bend against the forces outside of our control. Flexibility is similar to adaptability. Bending instead of breaking allows us the opportunity to meet our purpose even after we move out of positions of greatness. Flexibility is being adaptable so our potential can be reached. I will talk more about this later in the book, but this is a core value that I want to always teach my kids and as many people as possible. If you're inflexible, you can't survive and adapt.

Focus: Focus is the gift that enables you to evaluate and ask yourself, "Where is my balance? Where is my endurance? Where is my flexibility?" Focus enables you to realign yourself and to recalibrate your core values, enabling you to be stronger. Focus is a process in which you break down everything into smaller pieces, and then focus, brings it all together.

Everyone must ask themselves, "How do I utilize all of this for my greatest good?"

Suppose you decided to make a cake. You can have all the ingredients, but each separately won't make the cake. They must be combined and mixed in the right portions for the cake to come out right and be edible. It's important to note that you can have lots of individual ingredients, but if you don't have the right methods, you won't get the right results.

YES/NO
Describe

Detail

List

Confirm

YES/NO
Describe

Detail

List

Confirm

By taking all of the individual pieces that you have been building and bringing them together, you can get your intended outcome.

Strength: Strength is the product of all these steps, all these components maximized and brought together. Never chase what you desire; chase the components of what you desire. When you have a grasp of the components of what you desire, the thing you desire will bend to your will.

The secret to obtaining results is to gain specialized knowledge (components) and applying that knowledge to obtain a specific purpose. Your strengths are the gift of your efforts. As your gift, your strength can be used as you see fit. How can we all encourage our loved ones to build strength?

In the gym there's a term you've probably heard: no pain, no gain. If you work out, you know what I'm talking about. You work your biceps, or you do squats, and then you start to feel pain the next day or the day after. Is there something wrong? No, of course not. The athlete who is looking to gain muscle size and strength knows that there will be pain. In fact, he welcomes it. No pain, no gain. That pain is simply the muscle expanding, repairing and growing itself. The more effort you put into the workout results in more pain, which results in more growth and strength. The process of exercise requires your muscles to be torn down. The only way your muscles can grow is for them to be pushed to failure and broken down.

This is the same process for any growth in life. Strength is developed through the pain of reaching our limits and through the effects of conquered adversity.

In the chapters that follow, I'll talk a lot more about my core values and how I define success, but it's different for each individual. My core values aren't yours. You can definitely lean from them if you are searching for yours, but I would tell you to seek yourself to find what is true to you.

YES/NO

Describe

Detail

List

Confirm

Notes

CHAPTER 3

BALANCE

Balance, at its core, is the understanding that there is both positive and negative energy. Finding the balance and the middle ground between these two energies is critical. You must understand how to begin and to begin with the end in mind. **What must you pull yourself toward, and what must you push through in order to grasp your purpose and meet your objectives?**

I have been diving into these concepts and wondering what image would best illustrate the core values I have laid out for you, and I think it's the pyramid. The foundation of the pyramid is balance. Everything builds upon the foundation of balance. A pyramid starts with a wide base and slowly progresses until it creates

YES/NO

Describe

Detail

List

Confirm

YES/NO
Describe

Detail

List

Confirm

a pointed top. At the top of the pyramid is strength. Strength is the point of the spear. The point of the spear is the portion of the spear used to thrust into an opponent. The opponent represents any situation where you impose your will.

So, understanding that balance is the foundation upon which everything else is built, the question that may enter your mind is, **"What makes up balance? What are the ingredients that make it possible?"**

Similar to building a house, the first thing you need is a firm foundation. When building a structure, the cost of the foundation is the most expensive part of the project, but it is never seen. Think about that; the most expensive portion of any building is hidden from sight. No different, the most important part of you is hidden from plain sight.

Around 2001 I was blessed to find the martial art of Jeet Kune Do. This martial art taught me the difference between strength and power. It was a gym with no belts. The process of ranking was simple and subtle but definitely effective. At the beginning and ending of each class, we bowed in and out, from right to left, the most experienced to the least experienced. At any time that you believed you were standing in the wrong place, you moved and stood where you believed you belonged. If the person you stood in front of thought you had made a mistake, the bowing in and out of class was stopped, and we found out the true order of things. An atmosphere like this creates the most genuine experiences because there is no room for posturing or posing.

My Sifu Master Willie Wilson III once gave me a lesson on power that I have never forgotten. One day the class and I were punching heavy bags and doing mitt work. While I was training, my ego made me believe I was hitting the bag and mitts extremely hard. Sifu Wilson watched and said nothing. I knew he was watching, so I began punching the bag as hard as I could. He broke the silence and said, "Germaine, if you ever learned how to punch, you might do some damage one day," and walked off. In my mind, I said, "Whatever! I'm killing this bag!" I guess my body language communicated the same message.

Sifu Wilson saw this and instructed me to go get three telephone books from his desk. I did, and Sifu instructed me to hold the telephone books against my chest and sternum. Sifu then placed his open hand against the books, touching them with the tips of his fingers. He closed his fist, and from one inch away,

YES/NO

Describe

Detail

List

Confirm

YES/NO
Describe

Detail

List

Confirm

hit me so hard that I was knocked across the room and off my feet. Had I not placed the phone books against my sternum, he would have at the least bruised it or worse. I had never seen such power and force applied in such a small space. I later found out that was called the one-inch punch.

Sifu later explained that my punches looked and sounded like someone hitting a blunt object with a bat, *boom boom boom*. He said in order to draw power, instead imagine a bat connected at the end with a chain and at the end of the chain a solid metal ball. The sound that weapon would make would be *whaaaaaaaap*, and it would strike much harder because of the speed and power generated by the chain and ball. "Germaine, power is always created by flexible leverage, never by brute strength. Power is the transportation of strength. In order to be powerful, you must be willing to redistribute strength into flexible motion that is focused."

Your body is the bat, your arm is the chain, and your fist is the metal ball connected to the chain. Power is not generated from your hand, arm, or even your body. Power is generated from your foundation. From the earth, through your feet, through your hips, and dispersed. Our foundation—the sources of our power—always comes from our ability to manage our balance and stability.

Likewise, a building with bad plumbing, doors, walls, and even a bad roof can be repaired. But if the foundation is broken, the building is condemned. The building is unfit for human inhabitance. We must take our time in building the foundations we stand on.

Foundations, these days, are made from concrete. Concrete is made up of three primary ingredients: cement, water, and aggregates (sand and crushed stone). Without these ingredients, you cannot make concrete . Balance is also made up of different ingredients, and without them you will not achieve balance. Let's touch on the ingredients to balance, and then we can talk about balance itself. I think that approach will help you better understand balance, at least from my perspective.

The first, and perhaps most critical ingredient, is character.

The question of making decisions based on provisions rather than purpose is a question of character. Decisions based solely on provisions without connection to purpose will always result in a lapse in character. Character is challenged the moment we choose provisions

YES/NO
Describe

Detail

List

Confirm

YES/NO
Describe

Detail

List

Confirm

over purpose. More plainly, any time we choose to satisfy one of the three temptations seated in appetite, power, or pride over our purpose, we sacrifice our character for the provision. Our actions articulate that the provision is our master and our purpose is our second. When we use persons, places, and things outside their purpose, we inevitably abuse them. Likewise, we cheapen our character by making decisions solely on provisions and inevitably abuse ourselves.

The Bible narrative of Adam and Eve in the Garden of Eden speaks to this fact. Humanity lost its place in Eden when man lost his character. The character of man was lost as he traded the truth of his purpose for the provision of knowledge. It is possible to have all the knowledge and facts without an ounce of the truth. Every day innocent people go to jail while guilty people are set free based on the way facts and knowledge about a case are argued. The character of man was to live and make decisions based on the relationship of truthful understanding.

We identify letters, numbers, and statues as characters. We call them characters because the letter A is always A, the number 3 is always 3; the facial expressions, stance, and engraving on a statue are always the same. Likewise, our character is identified by what people can expect from us

What can the world expect from you?

When mentoring a CEO or even a young person, I stress to them how their gift can lead them somewhere that their character cannot sustain them. For example, you may have this ultra-high gifting that elevates you to a certain level. However, once you get there, you can't sustain it because your character doesn't match your gift.

During my first training as an official team member, my team leader, a Texas Ranger named Brad, told a story. Brad was a great leader; his passion and integrity inspired me. He is definitely one of the people I think about when I lead. The story was a call to action and set the stage for his expectation of character. As the day began, I was excited to prove myself to my teammates. Brad called for me and another young team member.

"Gas Can, Bubbles." We all had nicknames we acquired by our efforts either during tryouts, training, and missions. Your nickname was a testament to your character. I was called Gas Can. Gas Can was a take on my last name, and it spoke to the fact that I was always willing to go. I was full of energy and ready to rock and roll when called upon, whether we

YES/NO
Describe

Detail

List

Confirm

Y E S / N O
Describe

Detail

List

Confirm

were cleaning equipment or the barracks or prepping to take a hill. I would later receive a second name, The Navigator, because I got lost a couple of times in rural Texas on our way to training. Our names always had meaning, and most times they were laced with comedy.

Brad told us to sit down, and he told us this story:

Gents, a couple of years back I was working the border. I was in a mobile unit riding with a team member and a local liaison. All of a sudden, we received word over the radio that one of our teams that was lying in along the river bed was taking fire and being overrun by a narco-terrorist human trafficking organization. We whipped the car around and started heading toward the fight. During the drive, the vehicle, an off-road four-by-four jeep, caught a flat. My teammate and I jumped out and continued motivating to the fight. The fight was about a mile-and-a-half away. We were both carrying our weapons and packs, easily seventy to eighty pounds. A half-mile into the run toward the fight, the liaison fell to his knees and said, "My friend, my friend, continue without me. I can't run any farther." We did, and all was well for the guys that needed help. After that event, the liaison that fell out was named after the *Austin Powers* character Fat Bastard.

After telling the story, Brad screamed at us and said, "Don't ever be that guy! He failed us because he didn't train and prepare on sunny days like today for the fight when it's dark cold and wet! Don't be that guy!"

Does your character match your gift?

Do the people who know you intimately expect the same results from your gift that they expect from you as a person?

Do you practice the same way you play the game?

Integrity is another crucial ingredient for balance.

Integrity is the integrating and aligning of your mind, spirit, and speech, which is then exemplified through your actions. Integrity, simply put, is the matching of your heart, thoughts, and actions. Being integrated—being in line

YES/NO
Describe

Detail

List

Confirm

YES/NO
Describe

Detail

List

Confirm

with our true self—allows us to be grace-ful. This is no different than speaking of the integrity of a building. When asking a question of structural integrity of a build-ing, we are asking whether the building is constructed in a way that will allow it to stand fast in the face of adverse pres-sure and weather. Likewise, our integrity speaks to the alignment of our characters and virtues to stand against adverse con-ditions and storms.

During Hurricane Rita, I was assigned to a strike team that traveled anywhere in the state of Texas affected by Hurricane Rita that needed immediate assistance prior to, during, and post-Hurricane Rita. During the mission I found myself in Beaumont, Texas, for several days. While working this detail, there was no electricity or running water. During the state of emergency, a gas line was rup-tured, and there were no city or county workers available to repair or seal the broken line. It was a very dangerous time. While working my patrol, a teammate and I found a couple of boys walking out of a grocery store. They had broken into a store and were carrying lighter fluid, charcoal, water, and meat.

I relay this story because I want to measure it against balance, rather the ingredients of balance: character, and integrity. Character as I have defined it is purpose over provision. During this catastrophic event, the purpose for every human being was to stay alive. My role as an officer during this time of emergency was to assist with keeping people safe and alive. I ask you, were these boys challenging their character by taking food water and a means to prepare them during this time of extreme circumstance?

Was their integrity being challenged? Did their minds, heart, and spirit become misaligned by their actions?

My answer was to allow them to go uninterrupted. I found the same boys in a neighborhood hours later with multiple grills cooking and serving food throughout the community. Balance is not a fifty-fifty platform; it is the maintaining of the push and pull to create right action

Earlier, I identified integrity as being integrated—being in line with your true self—which allows us to be graceful. To many, the word *grace* has nothing to do with integrity. Oftentimes, when we speak of grace, we think of a euphoric feeling or the blaring of trumpets before some grand proclamation. That kind of imagery typically comes from religion, but the deeper meaning of grace is more profound. The original meaning of grace

YES/NO

Describe

Detail

List

Confirm

YES/NO
Describe

Detail

List

Confirm

in its Hebrew, Aramaic, or Greek origins is actually weightiness.

Weightiness is something that weighs so heavily upon you internally that it is seen externally. When something weighs upon you internally, it means it has made an impression on you. For example, your mother or father says something to you that was so deep and meaningful that it makes an imprint on your soul. This is what is meant when you say someone is impressive. Something about them puts a kind of pressure upon you internally, leaving an imprint so that your actions mirror what has been impressed upon you. This is the true meaning of grace. So, when you say, "I'm walking in grace," you are saying that your life is reflecting that which was imprinted upon your spirit. Likewise, when we identify a dancer, actor, speaker, or whomever as being graceful in their craft, we are communicating that the time spent training for their specific craft is evident in their delivery.

The reason why I define these words and include them as ingredients that make up balance is because balance, in essence, is *you*. Too often people live their entire lives without being introduced to themselves.

Dave Grossman, author and retired lieutenant colonel in the United States

Army, speaks of there being three types of people in the world. He says that 98 percent of people are sheep. One percent are wolves, and the remaining one percent are sheepdogs. Sheep keep their heads down, graze wherever, and go wherever they are guided or even misguided. Sheep make up the largest part of the world's population. The wolves prey upon the sheep because sheep do not pay attention to what's going on around them. Wolves have an appetite for destruction; they desire to steal, kill, and destroy, and sheep make for easy targets. Lastly, there are the sheepdogs. Sheepdogs protect the sheep from the wolves. Sheepdogs and wolves are similar in that they will not run away from conflict.

The sheepdog relishes a righteous fight. The only difference between the wolf and the sheepdog is the moral standing of the sheepdog. The sheepdog desires to protect and cultivate and will kill to do so. I take Dave Grossman's interpretation of society one step further and say the 98 percent who are sheep are sheep because they have an oppressed mindset. They are oppressed because they are not true to themselves. They have not opened up to themselves, and neither have they found their purpose (and therefore will not find balance). For them, it's easier to

YES/NO

Describe

Detail

List

Confirm

simply follow the group. It's easier to be oppressed than it is to be free.

There are three mindsets: oppressed, delivered, and renewed.

Oppressed mindsets find security in slavery because the security of slavery is the absence of responsibility. I'm not speaking of slavery in the terms of physical bondage but rather mental bondage and servitude. This form of slavery embraces bondage over personal responsibility. **So you must ask yourself, "Am I being responsible in this moment, or am I seeking security in something that is not real?"** Remember, the security of slavery is the absence of responsibility. The comfort of an oppressed mindset is the absence of self-determination. Examine yourself and see if you are self-determined. **Where are you in the grand scheme of things? Are you being responsible? Are you demonstrating self-determination?** The attraction of subjugation is the privilege of blame, meaning if things go wrong, you can point the finger at someone other than yourself. So wherever I see blame, I also see a lack of self-examination and responsibility. Blame is a fruit born from the seed of an oppressed mindset. The only way possible for us to carry out the mission is freedom in our thinking.

Before you can be free and truly see and understand yourself, you must relinquish anything hindering your ability to carry out your ability to be responsible. Irresponsibility is another way of saying lack of personal accountability. It is being comfortable with fickleness, inconsistency, and letting things slide.

In order to create the foundation of balance, you must be willing to walk away from irresponsibility and stop placing the blame elsewhere. Regardless of the situation, you are the author of your own story. You get to decide what role you play in the story of your life. If you choose to keep an oppressed mindset, you will have to ask yourself if you are truly committed to your vision.

Vision can be defined as your purpose in pictures. Our visions are always perfect because they are the high-definition panoramic views of the perfect future. Our faith is the engine that propels the journey of where we stand to what we see in our visions. Often, we allow our sight to be the enemy of our vision, believing in the facts we see rather than trusting in the truth of our vision's potential.

Earlier, I spoke of a special ops mission my team and I conducted. During that mission, we only physically saw our target, the compound resting on the thirty

YES/NO
Describe

Detail

List

Confirm

YES/NO
Describe

Detail

List

Confirm

acres of land, once we had acquired the suspect. Prior to that we only saw aerial photos and pictures of the compound. Those aerial photos and pictures gave us a vision of what we were looking for. The pictures were our vision, our purpose in pictures.

You may take this journey, visualizing your purpose, and determine that you have an oppressed mindset. If so, the question then becomes, "How do I deliver myself from this oppressed state?" This task can only be accomplished without ego. You can't be in a place of self-righteousness. Negative thoughts and behavior must be replaced with a positive reinforcing action. You can't fall into the usual traps of "I'm just not going to think this anymore" or "I'm not going to do this because I'm better than that." Those thought processes are ego-driven thinking. They are based on the faulty premise that you alone, without a detailed working system or plan, are enough. A success-driven thought process values follow-through and planning. The process of creating a plan creates value and understanding and makes you enough to fight for the right to be free. Thinking about what we are not going to do is no different than leaving our foot- and handprints in the sand. The print will disappear and be filled with sand once again. Once we redirect a thought, we must replace it with an action thought. The action thought must be preprogrammed. This action thought takes the place of the negative thought and positively charges us into the direction we want to go.

The idea is to visualize the gap between where you are and where you want to be. You have to figure out how to make that journey. You must grasp the fact that even though you are self-aware enough to realize you must deliver yourself from an oppressed mindset to a renewed mindset, you are still the same person and possess the same mind. Rebuilding that mind is the course of action we now begin. The right answer can only follow the right question. That is why we always begin with a question:

"What am I thinking about?"

Growing up, all my couches told me, "Defense wins championships," and for years I thought this was merely a cliché until I was taught what it truly meant. It is impossible to defend something not already in your possession. The idea of "defense wins championships" stems from the reality that we are already champions.

YES/NO

Describe

Detail

List

Confirm

YES/NO
Describe

Detail

List

Confirm

This is important because you become what you think about the most. We think about the things we allow to consume us. Pause here and think about what you think about most. **Write down what five things you think about most.** These five things are what you allow yourself to be consumed by. When delivering yourself from an oppressed mindset, your thoughts must continually constitute responsibility, self-determination, and self-accountability. **Are the five things you wrote in line with what you say you value?** If not, your thoughts are oppressing the very things, ideas, and people you value. When the stories and words you play and replay in your mind match your visions, your deliverance mindset is in action.

During one of my relationships there were situations to which I did not like how I responded. I felt that I responded weakly, and the idea of being weak bothered me. I would relive these situations and play thoughts in my mind of how I would have rather responded. As I matured, I had to ask why I chose to replay these specific thoughts. I noticed the abundancy of negative feelings I experienced by replaying them. So why did I do it? I did it because I had not moved past the situations. It became difficult not to dive into the obsess of negativity. That negativity reeked from

YES/NO
Describe

Detail

List

Confirm

my pores. By replacing those thoughts with positive thoughts or mantras, I grew past the hang-up and delivered my mind from the effects of negativity. Remember, we become what we think about most. We think about the things we allow to consume us. Righteous thoughts become right action.

Once you have created your vision and are being drawn toward it, you will be tested. Life will always test your convictions. Nearly all tests can be summarized into three categories: appetite, power, and pride. As you process life with a renewed mind, you will be able to go through these tests by asking yourself the right questions.

"What am I looking at? What is my test in this situation? What is my appetite seeking? Is my appetite under control?" Appetite here is referring to your physical appetites, vices that you indulge in. **You may also ask yourself, "Is this decision on power or me obtaining power? Is it a decision made to empower my purpose or receive the power of reward? Is it centered on empowering those around me for the result of a greater good?"**

Finally, there are tests of pride. Pride is synonymous with ego. "I want to identify myself as this. I want to be seen in this way."

YES/NO
Describe

Detail

List

Confirm

One of the things that I learned when I was speaking in front of people is that if I'm concerned about how I look and sound, I become nervous. That's pride. However, if I am more concerned about positively impacting others or whom I am helping, my nervousness goes away. The reason for that is I am shifting my focus off myself and onto others. Consider this: **How nervous are you when you are giving a gift to someone else?** You're not because you're giving to another and not concerned about yourself.

Remember that this process is about identifying where you are at any given moment; it's about being fully present and self-aware. Before the GPS can tell you where to go, it must locate where you are. This is the building of your foundation of balance, and balance is *you*.

This is a crucial part of your growth. On this journey you will discover that there are three stages of growth:

1. You're heading toward a test.

2. You're already going through a test.

3. You're on the other side of a test.

If you are heading toward a test, pause and evaluate your mindset. You are the author of your own thoughts, and you can summarize how something will end based on what you're thinking. If you're inside of a test, it's the same thing. **What is your mindset?** You will bring to pass that which you focus on. As you come out the other side of a test, you have to ask yourself, **"Did I *go* through that, or did I *grow* through that?"** *Going* through the test is just going through the motions and enduring it. The same test is sure to come again. But if you were *growing* through it, you were learning how to solve the problem. Then, when you encounter it again, it is no longer a problem. **When was the last time you figured out what one plus one was?** But when a kindergartner or preschooler is asked that question, it becomes a process of figuring. Make every concern an opportunity and your opportunities your future one-plus-ones.

To find yourself is to lose your footing. Growth requires failure, and failure is never final, unless you allow it to be. So, losing your footing and moving forward is just part of the process.

I find peace and comfort inside my purpose. You can look around and find people who are going through the motions, doing things only because they think they should or worse, because

YES/NO

Describe

Detail

List

Confirm

YES/NO
Describe

Detail

List

Confirm

someone else thinks they should. They hope to get fulfillment, and maybe they receive a shallow facsimile of it, but it won't bring happiness. True success is impossible to be had without happiness and fulfilment.

In order to find your balance, you must ask yourself the right questions. As a youth, I watched kung fu theater, and many of the characters spoke in parables similar to Jesus and other teachers. Parable teaching is rooted in the understanding that nothing is yours until you understand it, not even yourself. The reason we ask questions of ourselves is to better learn about ourselves. The answering of these questions gives us the material (knowledge) that allows us to understand ourselves. That understanding allows us to act in wisdom. It is foolish to be wise about everything outside of ourselves. **How can we truly know, love, or appreciate others until we do the same for ourselves?**

The first ingredient mentioned was character. I've had some experiences in recent years that helped build my character. I had to ask myself questions like, **"What is most important, being fair, being just, and is doing the right thing always doing the good thing?"**

The story I shared earlier regarding Hurricane Rita helped me find my balance and build my foundation.

When Hurricane Rita hit Texas and I was placed on the strike team, there was little to no expectation of assistance. The men on the strike team were the only backup we would have for the next seven to ten days. When a problem arose, we were mobilized and sent directly to the location in order to handle the situation. We were sent to a multitude of places. Once we arrived at a location and handled the issue, we were sent somewhere else. While everyone else was driving northbound on Highway 45, we were the only people southbound. We slept in the cold and in jails, our cars, and even on high school floors. The hotels were all closed due to flooding, and the area was being evacuated, so bed and breakfasts weren't available. (Imagine that: during a major evacuation and mass flooding no bed and breakfast!) For several nights we resided in the city of Huntsville in the Walker County Jail. The sheriff at the time was a retired Texas Ranger, and he provided food and shelter for us when we had opportunities to rest. We slept in jail cells, took communal showers, and were fed by the trustee staff. It was a humbling experience. We walked inside the county

YES/NO
Describe

Detail

List

Confirm

YES/NO
Describe

Detail

List

Confirm

jail and heard the sound of the jail doors closing. The cells doors stayed open, but the doors to the areas we resided were locked down. However, I must admit we were all so tired at the day's end I couldn't tell you much other than both food and sleep were luxuries.

The motto of the Texas Department of Public Safety is Courtesy, Service, and Protection. All three characteristics are put to the test in extreme circumstances. Question: Was it fair that we were driving toward the hurricane when everyone else was driving the opposite direction? Absolutely not. Was it the right thing to do? Absolutely *yes*. Without our presence, there were many people who would have been severely injured or lost their lives. My thoughts had to be focused on my responsibilities and on what needed to be done. My focus gave me balance and allowed me to support the team and the mission and created the best opportunity to come home.

During the hurricane evacuation we found ourselves in Huntsville. Another trooper and I were tasked to secure a gasoline truck parked in the middle of a Walmart parking lot. Most of the gas stations from Houston to Dallas had no gas to provide evacuees. The Texas Department of Transportation stepped in and gave gasoline to motorists who were stranded or running low on fuel. Naturally, there was chaos. Sixty or more carloads of people surrounded the tanker, all desperate for gasoline and demanding it.

Our team leader ordered the other trooper and I to the parking lot. It was just the two of us because the rest of the team was engaged somewhere else. Our orders were to secure the tanker, get it back on the highway, and keep it safe. We made our way to the tanker, established a command presence, and demonstrated a firm and fair hand. We had to secure the tanker and keep everyone safe. We achieved that by providing a certain amount of fuel to each vehicle. Now, there was no doubt that some people needed more fuel than others, depending on how far they were driving. Due to the nature of the circumstances, we didn't have the luxury of deciphering who needed what, so we issued what we determined was a "fair" amount. Once again, balance was achieved by being present and asking the right questions for the situation.

With regard to Beaumont, the city that had no water, no electricity, and a gas leak during Hurricane Rita, the entire city was shut down. The gas leak I mentioned earlier would be dangerous enough during a normal shift, but during a hurricane

YES/NO
Describe

Detail

List

Confirm

YES/NO
Describe

Detail

List

Confirm

evacuation, it became more dangerous due to lacks in resources and manpower. We assisted the local police department with twenty-four-hour patrols. During a night patrol, a teammate and I encountered a group of kids who had just broken into a grocery store. They saw us and ran from the building. We caught them and sat them down and started evaluating what was going on. The kids had stolen charcoal, lighter fluid, meat, eggs, potatoes, and milk from the store. Was it fair that they were taking items from the grocery store without paying for it? Absolutely not. But was it justified? Absolutely *yes*! Based on the environment, the conditions, and the law of self-preservation, these kids were scavenging for necessities. During our interview of the kids, we found that they were not only scavenging for themselves but for their families and other elderly persons in their neighborhood that were all holding up together. **Where is the balance in this scenario? What would you do, as either the officer or the person attempting to survive!** There are moments in your life when you have to seek righteousness, not fairness. It's not like they were stealing new televisions. They were stealing food and supplies that would save lives. The boy's purpose and intent were the balancing factor that measured their integrity. The supreme law of survival over the civil rule of theft and vandalism. Integrity is the alignment of divine and natural purpose. Purpose purifies us from self-pity, blame, and lacks in accountability.

Later, we actually found some guys who were looting and stealing televisions. They were handled in a completely different way. Two similar yet different situations that required balance to resolve. When traveling from one destination to another, there are always multiple routes to take. All the routes are "good" routes as long as they get you to your destination. But the right route gets you to your destination on time with the least amount of strain and in working condition. The good thing or way is not always the right way. Balance is finding the right way— the way that fits your time, ability, and condition as you travel to your purpose.

I shared these examples in order to illustrate balance. In each scenario I had to ask questions, determine what was right, what was needed, and then act.

Question: **Is God, *God* because he knows all things or because he always knows the right thing? How often do we have all the information and make the wrong choice?** I believe God is God because he always knows the *right* thing.

YES/NO

Describe

Detail

List

Confirm

YES/NO
Describe

Detail

List

Confirm

Right action is a product of right thought. As we travel the road of life, perfection is unattainable. True perfection is unnatural; there are no straight lines or perfect circles in nature.

We had to learn how to make sufficient hiding spaces. While conducting missions on the Texas–Mexico border, we were often tasked to work inside listening and observations posts (LPOPs). LPOPs required us to insert ourselves with a teammate into different places under the veil of darkness or cover for the purpose of collecting intelligence and to relay information about the movements of narco-terrorists and other criminal elements. We hid using sniper tactics and personal-made ghillie suits for days at a time. It is impossible to create a hide or ghillie suit capable of hiding from human detection if straight lines can be seen within either the suit or the hiding space; perfection and straight lines do not exist in nature. Straight lines are a manmade creation. It is our imperfections that make us perfect for the environment we live in.

What is attainable is perfect effort and perfect intent. In this way, you will find balance.

Imagine being on a balancing beam. What keeps you on that beam are small inputs of both pushing and pulling positive and negative energy. The amount of pressure used to maintain your balance is often not fifty-fifty. No, it's based on the environment and the last commitments made to stay afloat. Sometimes the wind is blowing, and if the wind is blowing you from one side, then you will have to lean into the wind in order to stay balanced. Finding your balance is a matter of understanding, being in the present, and knowing your purpose.

It is important to note that when you are ego driven, you cannot achieve balance. Here is an example to demonstrate the difference between being driven by ego and not being driven by ego. Let's say you are a parent. You can view this role in terms of "I desire to be a good parent. If I do this or that, it will help me to become the best parent I can be." This statement attaches your actions to the adding or subtracting to the consistent identity of "I am a good parent."

An ego-driven view is quite different. The ego-driven view ties you to a constant state of proving. Within this mindset, all self-action must prove or disprove the person as being a good parent. In other words, "parent" takes on the identity of the person rather than a role the person plays in their life. So from the ego-driven perspective, if someone were to make suggestions to you on how to be

YES/NO
Describe

Detail

List

Confirm

YES/NO

Describe

Detail

List

Oonfirm

a good parent, you would be offended and feel your worth had been questioned. When people take on an identity as their true selves, any action that questions what they are doing becomes an assault on their person, and they usually fight like they're fighting for their life, no matter how small the issue. They do so because their ego is telling them their very existence as a parent or any other role is being attacked, and if they lose this fight, they cannot exist as what they perceive themselves to be. **Have you ever met someone who was defensive about everything?** They may feel as if their ego is being attacked when it's not, or they're unteachable and unwilling to listen to another point of view.

The ego-driven person lives for validation. They live in a world where everything they do has to receive some kind of validation. The validation proves to them that their idea of themselves is true. An individual with a success-driven mindset needs no validation. They seek only to increase their knowledge and wisdom so that they can always be living in alignment with their purpose and be in balance. The key to being balanced is to get to the point where you're open enough to see who you are and where you want to be while also using the skills and resources around you to get to your destination. That's not attainable without understanding who you are and where you are. If you don't know who you are, you cannot shift out of an oppressive mindset. If you don't know where you are, you won't know where to go, much less how to get there, which brings us back to the questions we asked at the beginning of this chapter.

What must you pull yourself toward, and what must you push through in order to grasp your purpose and meet your objectives? Remember that balance is about who you are. It's your character and your integrity .

YES/NO
Describe

Detail

List

Confirm

Notes

CHAPTER 4

ENDURANCE

Endurance, in simple terms, can be defined as how much energy is consistently exerted toward a goal before one becomes completely drained of energy. We live in time only because we haven't made it to eternity.

Our physical body comes with an expiration date. We need to know how to sustain enough energy to push through our limitations in order to live the entire span of our lifetime. It is important to note here the difference between *endure* and *endurance*. To endure something means to suffer through it. You go through a hard time, make it through, and then look back on it as something you survived. Endurance, however, speaks more to the state of mind with which you endured the

YES/NO
Describe

Detail

List

Confirm

YES/NO
Describe

Detail

List

Confirm

challenge . Understand that the mindset with which you go through something is far more important than what you actually go through.

Late one morning during the special ops qualification process, after that morning's departmental physical testing that we were required to pass with a score of 90 percent or better with only a couple of hours of sleep, we stood at attention in front of a railroad tie. The railroad tie was about twelve feet long and weighed around 350 pounds. The cadre for the evaluation told six of us to pick it up. We stood looking at each other and had to devise a plan on how to pick the railroad tie up together. The idea of picking up the log was simple, but as a team we had to coordinate our efforts. This required communication—communication while being yelled at, flashbanged, and gassed. Another day at the office. So we picked it up with no problem. All six on one side, with the railroad tie resting on our shoulders.

He yelled, "There are eight different teams of six here. Every team has a railroad tie!" As the other teams split up and hoisted their railroad tie, he added, "We're going for a walk. This training evolution has designated timed hacks (required time designated to meet each section of the walk); don't ask how long each section is. Just walk! You must make the designated time for each section. You need to make the time! Make the time! It pays to be first!" he yelled and started walking.

We began walking, and we walked and walked. It was August, and the temperature hovered around 110 degrees. We walked under pine trees, and inside that forest it felt more like 115 degrees. It took physical endurance to make it through that. There was a time when I stopped thinking about action and focused only on making that next step, and then the next step. I was no longer focused on the heat. I only focused on that next step and the sound of my teammates on the log with me. We walked in a line, and I was at the head of the line. My position made me the point. However, I could not see anyone on the log with me. The person at the rear was the leader by position because he saw all the moving parts. As we walked, we had to find a cadence that allowed us to move in step. Secondly, we had to communicate when, where, and how we would transfer the log from the left to right shoulder. We all had varied heights, strengths, and so on, so communication was key. My focus became less on what I needed and more on what the

YES/NO
Describe

Detail

List

Confirm

team needed. In order to know what the team needed, I had to drown out my own thoughts and hear the commands given from the rear. While doing so, I also had to navigate the ship and control the speed of the log—this was a race after all, and it pays to be first!

Mantras are useful when it comes to your mental endurance. What you articulate to your subconscious will eventually show up in your actions, and it will also dictate how much mental endurance you have.

Often, our endurance is compromised not by our ability but by the internal story we tell ourselves.

Your brain is no different than the hard drive of a computer. Things that come through the input of your five senses are downloaded to your subconscious. What you see, smell, taste, feel, and hear all get downloaded to your brain. When the input is repetitive for a long enough time, it becomes embedded in your sub-conscious. What gets embedded in your subconscious will come out of you when pressed or stressed, much like an automated program on a computer. You can use this to your advantage.

Your mental, or psychological, endurance is directly proportional to the things you tell yourself subconsciously over and over. It is tied directly to your self-concept. You can affect this by programming your "hard drive," or subconscious, with your self-talk and with mantras.

My mantras sound like this: "I'm a *beast!*" Sometimes it's "I can't lose; even if I'm down, I'm catching up," or "Hard work, *easy work.*" Whenever people greet me with "Hey, how are you doing?" I immediately answer, "Outstanding!" It's up to me, and it's my choice how I respond regardless of what's going on in my life at that moment. I choose how I see myself.

Psychological endurance is similar to the muscles in your body in that it must be exercised and maintained in order for it to be strong. It is important to maintain both mental and physical endurance, and you do this by continually challenging yourself. If you desire to make it to the next level, you must push yourself beyond your current level of capabilities. Building physical endurance is, in many ways, a straightforward endeavor It requires a systematic exercise regimen, with increased levels of difficulty applied in incremental steps.

Psychological endurance is a bit more complex. Physical endurance training is a key component of psychological endurance because it helps you to develop

YES/NO
Describe

Detail

List

Confirm

YES/NO
Describe

Detail

List

Confirm

laser-like focus, but there's more to it. You need to strengthen your ability to handle psychological stress and manage your reactions to it so that you can maintain a high level of performance .

When the topic of psychological endurance comes up, I think of Pop (my grandfather). Often, when asked how he was doing, he'd answer, "Fighting the bear, baby!" The comment came from a saying I always heard him say: "If you ever see me in the woods fighting a bear, help the m-f-ing bear, cause I'm about to get 'em." That always made an impact on me because I knew what my grandfather had been through in his life. He had been a sharecropper, and he experienced the realities of slavery. He would get paid a meager salary to do work. Then, at the end of each week, he would be charged for the use of the tools he used, the place where he slept, and even the food he ate. The bill always came to more money than what he had made from the work, so he was always in debt. It was modern-day slavery. After sharecropping, he did many different things. He worked for a railroad, hustled, gambled, and did several odd jobs.

Eventually, he saved enough money to purchase a home for his wife and five children. When he passed, he left my grandmother enough money to live comfortably until she passed with no debt.

Now, when you ask a guy like that how he's doing and he says, "Fighting the bear, and I'm about to get him," what level of mental endurance do you think he has **Where does his mental fortitude and resilience come from?** Despite his circumstances and ongoing challenges, he maintained his focus and kept "fighting the bear." He reached a high level of mental toughness because he exercised his endurance for years. That is self-management. He took responsibility for his own behavior and well-being. Growth requires self-management, and without it there is no growth. As you grow, so does your endurance.

These things are inherent within you and are principles that, as you apply them to your life, cause your endurance to grow. Your endurance is super important because endurance is the vehicle we use to spend our most valuable commodity: *time*. All humans have twenty-four hours a day. The way we spend our twenty-four determines the amount of power we create.

A story to illustrate time and power:

There were two lumberjacks, one old and one young. The young lumber jack said, "Old man, I can cut ten times the

YES/NO
Describe

Detail

List

Confirm

YES/NO
Describe

Detail

List

Confirm

number of trees down as you in an eight-hour day. You're a has-been."

The older lumberjack said, "No, young man, I believe I can beat you pretty nicely because you're young and don't know much." So the lumberjacks put it to the test. The young lumberjack started out cutting logs at a furious pace. He stopped to look at the older man after a couple of hours and saw the older lumberjack sitting down. The younger man continued to cut wood at a furious pace and stopped again, and again the older lumberjack was sitting down. This went on the entire eight hours. At the end of the day, when the lumberjacks counted trees cut, the older lumberjack had far more trees cut. The younger man could not believe it. He said, "Every time I looked at you, you were sitting down; how did you cut more trees? The older lumberjack smiled and said, "I was sharpening my blade. The way I spent my eight hours allowed me to produce more power to cut more trees."

This and Sifu's lesson on punching teach that the way we govern our leverage and sharpness dictates the power and endurance we can produce

As humans, we try to gain power over our situation and circumstances. This is why people read horoscopes or do things like palm readings. The power that we need, which only comes from having balance and endurance, is the power to govern ourselves. Balance and endurance give us the power to govern our actions through our self-concept.

These concepts aren't only applicable to you as an individual. They apply equally to a business, large or small. Every business has a culture, and that culture's ability to endure challenges and obstacles are tied directly to the power (balance + endurance) within that culture. Just as in the life of an individual, a business must recognize that it is not a matter of *if* they will encounter challenges but *when* they will do so.

Earlier we discussed how your psychological endurance is directly related to what you feed your subconscious. One way to intentionally feed your subconscious stories that will empower you is using mantras. The more I work with transformational champions, the more I see the power of this technique. A mantra is simply a phrase that you repeat to yourself over and over. It is a story you tell yourself, and when I see my clients employ this method of programming their subconscious, it yields amazing results. Mantras assist the visualization process. In fact, mantras can be

YES/NO
Describe

Detail

List

Confirm

YES/NO

Describe

Detail

List

Confirm

a powerful aid to help you form a mental picture of the outcome you desire.

I remember reading about an Australian woman who was a researcher, and she performed an experiment using basketball players. She recruited some elite players and then broke them up into three groups for twenty minutes a day. One group played basketball for the full twenty-minute period. Another group did not play basketball at all. However, they visualized, in detail, what they were going to do as if they were on the court. The last group did absolutely nothing related to basketball. At the conclusion of the experiment, the three groups were tested for their performance. The last group, who did nothing basketball related, ranked the worst. The group that visualized but didn't actually touch a basketball were neck and neck with the group who actually played every day for twenty minutes. That experiment proved, without a doubt, the power of visualization.

A mantra is a form of visualization because when you repeat it over and over, you become that which you are speaking.

There will be times in your life when you can't see the road ahead. It is in these times that you must WIN. This acronym stands for *what's important now*, and it means that all you need to do in order to keep moving forward is focus on the next thing you have to do. That's it. There will be distractions and obstacles all around you, but you must focus on what to do next and nothing more—just like when I was doing the special operations test with the railroad tie. I had no idea where I was going or how long it would take. The instructors were popping off flash bangs, popping smoke, spraying us with water, and yelling commands. I had absolutely no idea where I was going, and neither did I have an understanding of what time I was supposed to be there. I just knew that I needed to get there, and it paid to be a winner. So rather than worrying about the destination, I only had to worry about my team and the next step, then the step after that, and so on.

When you can't see the path ahead, all you have to do is just step in the direction that you're supposed to go. Then take another step, then another, and another. Eventually you will be able to see where you're supposed to be. If you allow yourself to become bogged down with fear and doubt or become paralyzed by overthinking, you will destroy your mindset.

I see this when I am training recruits. It is my job to put them through real-life scenarios. What happens is that when the pressure is on, their stress becomes

YES/NO

Describe

Detail

List

Confirm

YES/NO
Describe

Detail

List

Confirm

overwhelming and they seize up. They become stuck because they're looking for the easy out or the best answer that will get them through the situation. They become so focused on trying to figure out how they will make it that they get stuck. Remember, a good answer now is better than the perfect answer too late . When I was carrying that railroad tie, my "good answer" was just taking that next step. There were other answers available, too. There were men all around me who were quitting and dropping out. That was their answer to the situation. I made it through because I maintained my focus on my team and my next step.

I instructed those recruits to find their own personal mantra. It could be "I'm okay, I can do this" or "Easy day. I can handle this. I got this!" I knew that if they could visualize themselves succeeding because they programmed their subconscious accordingly, they would make it through.

Remember, your psychological endurance can only be compromised if you feed negative, self-limiting stories to your subconscious.

Notes

_____

_____

_____

_____

_____

_____

_____

_____

_____

_____

_____

_____

_____

_____

_____

_____

_____

_____

_____

_____

_____

_____

_____

_____

CHAPTER 5
FLEXIBILITY

The only guarantees in life are change and death.

Therefore, seeking comfort in security or permanency is a false ideal. Your strength does not come from being secure. Your strength comes from your ability to adapt and be flexible . This is crucial because flexibility will position you to integrate balance and endurance with opportunity. Opportunities will come because flexibility allows you to grow and shape yourself in such a way that your natural gifts become more effective. Being flexible and able to adapt will actually create more opportunities for you. You will recognize and make use of the resources around you.

YES/NO

Describe

Detail

List

Confirm

For example, everything that is needed to make an iPhone, or even an airplane, was present during the age of the dinosaurs. What made it possible for these things to eventually be created? It was the ability to manage and manipulate the resources. It was the flexibility and adaptability of the mind that eventually made it possible for these technological wonders to come into being. Often the fear of flexibility comes from a deep-rooted fear of suffering.

We do everything we can to avoid suffering. However, if you look back over your life and identify times that caused you the most stress, you will see that, in most cases, they were times when you were the least flexible.

Being flexible does not mean you are passive or weak. In fact, it means quite the opposite. Being flexible makes you stronger. It is a powerful skill that enables you to better approach an ever-changing world. **Working to ensure that you maintain a mindset that keeps you in a state of adaptability isn't the easy way, but if you always take the easy way, what happens?** You become weak. Sometimes we believe the lie that by avoiding suffering we are doing ourselves a favor. However, the only way to become stronger is to allow for some form of suffering.

For instance, when a child is learning how to walk, they fall down many times. If you pick that child up every time they fall and carry them and continued to do that, what would be the outcome? You would end up with a fifteen-year-old kid with underdeveloped legs that are too weak to function. At that point, they would experience real suffering.

One area in my life in which I had to be become more flexible involved my daughter. She was ready to go into high school, and I was set on her attending a school that was very close to me. When we talked about it, she said, "I don't want to go to that school." I asked, "Why not? We already worked this out." After a moment of silence, she responded, "Your footprints are too big!" More silence, and then she continued, "Everywhere you go, you're *that guy*, and I'm just the daughter. I want to go somewhere where no one knows me."

At first, I was a little upset and questioned her, "How dare you not want to go? It's all set up for you. I know the people there. I've already talked to them about you attending, and I got your steps lined up. All you have to do is follow the program and you're going to be good." Some more silence, then she replied, "I don't want that program; it's not *my* program!"

YES/NO

Describe

Detail

List

Confirm

YES/NO
Describe

Detail

List

Confirm

So after initially being mad and a little hurt, I could see it. I stepped back and thought about it.

"What's my purpose for her?" My purpose for her is for her to be the highest version of herself possible.

"Can that be accomplished with her going somewhere else?" Yes. "Is it worth it for me to require her to attend the school of my choice and risk damaging our relationship?" No way. "Is she really acting like anyone other than me right now?" Man, I've recreated a feminine version of myself!

I had to rebalance and shift my focus. And you will, too. Everyone faces this recalibration moment in life. **In what way do you have to make a shift? How will you shift focus on your relationships as they change? How flexible are you when it comes to adapting to new business or life opportunities?**

My relationship with my daughter has changed. How? I don't walk her to school every day. I allow her to walk herself to school every day. She comes back and tells me, "Hey, Dad, this is what's going on. This is what I think. What do you think? Okay. I don't need your help. I'll tell you about what happened when I'm done." My willingness to be more flexible in this area of my life allowed one of my greatest dreams to come true. My daughter is growing into the young lady that I want her to be. That's one example where I learned to be more flexible .

Flexibility will help you gain wisdom because when unexpected situations arise, you will be able to adapt and figure out how to handle them. Think about it. **When was the last time you formulated a plan, implemented that plan, and everything went off without a hitch?** Nothing changed, went wrong, or did not work. It went down perfectly. While anything is possible, I'm guessing you're having trouble remembering that ever happening.

In the previous chapter we talked about the importance of mental endurance. Mental endurance isn't about having the brute strength to keep going regardless of the circumstances. It's about being flexible enough to change, modify, and adapt your plan so that you can keep going and accomplish your objective. Flexibility gives you the advantage. With it you will have the ability to adapt to situational demands, and more importantly, you will increase your effectiveness. Without it your worry, doubt, and fear will crush you.

Being psychologically flexible means the same as being physically flexible. It

YES/NO
Describe

Detail

List

Confirm

YES/NO
Describe

Detail

List

Confirm

means you are able to stretch and be pliable. Flexibility allows you to stretch, and stretching allows growth.

As parents and leaders, we want to hang on to the progress and achievements we've made and pour into others. It can be frustrating to see those who don't live up to their calling. Be flexible enough to watch them grow, and allow people to make their own mistakes and achieve their own victories through trial and error. No pain, no gain. Success is a journey.

Exercise:

Ask yourself, **"In what area of life can I strive to be more flexible?"**

Notes

_____

_____

_____

_____

_____

_____

_____

_____

_____

_____

_____

_____

_____

_____

_____

_____

_____

_____

_____

_____

_____

_____

_____

_____

_____

CHAPTER 6
FOCUS

What does it mean to have focus?

For our journey of purpose and throughout this book, we are talking about the gift of vision, the faith of moving toward an objective and the sustenance to achieve. Focus is sometimes defined as the ability to concentrate on an effort, but it's more than that. We've talked about balance, endurance, and flexibility and how those three components are needed if we are to build strength and succeed. However, how we direct or focus those components will determine how strong we become and whether we will be successful. Balance, endurance, and flexibility are the rays of the sun, and focus is the magnifying glass that directs those sunbeams into a super-hot pinpoint of energy.

YES/NO

Describe

Detail

List

Confirm

Y E S / N O
Describe

Detail

List

Confirm

No different than baking a cake, you can have all the ingredients, but if the application is not right then the outcome is not right . Having balance, endurance and flexibility is no different than obtaining information, but not having the wisdom to apply it. Once we understand how to focus our effort then we experience where our energy turns to synergy. Focus is the critical element of success.

Rather than one plus one equaling two, one plus one equals infinity through direct, focused effort. For example, I played college football when I was only seventeen years old. I played a lot my freshman year and became a starter my sophomore year. I was injured at the beginning of my junior year and missed half the games that year. Now, I was strong, fast, and aggressive, but those first couple of years I played from the vantage point of not losing. My focus was on the responsibility of my position. I wasn't going to let go of that responsibility and played it safe. Playing it safe made me an average player, or maybe a little above average. But my senior year, my vantage point changed.

After being injured, I tried to come back, and the coach thought I was trying to come back too soon. He said, "You're hesitating. We can't have you hesitating in your position. This is your position to lose, but you cannot play it hurt."

I went back to the drawing board and rehabbed both my knee and my mindset. When I took the field my senior year, I had my best year ever. The difference was I wasn't playing a position or area of the field; I was playing the game. My focus changed. My focus became a concentrated effort, and I experienced exponential growth in synergy. Like the tip of a sword, all the action, energy, and force pushed the tip of the sword in one direction, in one concerted effort.

Another example is when I was on the team performing a hit (raid) in law enforcement. Typically, a hit consists of the act of serving of a warrant to acquire persons, places, or things. A warrant requires the securing and/or acquiring of locations to be searched, the arresting of people, and at times both. We usually executed warrants in the dark of the morning. We use what's called a dynamic entry. What that means is that all the energy and focus is aimed at the front door of the building or house. It is one simultaneous effort with the single objective to be overwhelming so that when you go inside the home, you can acquire the person without a fight. It usually went down something like this: The

YES/NO

Describe

Detail

List

Confirm

YES/NO
Describe

Detail

List

Confirm

subject of the warrant has been asleep all night. It's four or five in the morning, then all of a sudden, *boom!* A breacher hits the front door. As the front door is hit, a flash bang goes off. *Bang, bang, bang, bang.* After the flash bangs, you have window teams breaking windows. So, you hear an explosion. You hear the breacher. You see people running through your house. There's a helicopter with lights hovering above the house. All this comes as you are asleep. You wake up, and you see all these men with guns pointing at you yelling, "Don't move!" The result, due to the overwhelming nature of dynamic action, is winning the fight without having to fight.

Talk about extreme focus!

That same kind of dynamic action happens when you focus balance, endurance, and flexibility to one specific item or one specific agenda. The rule in moving with focus is to not move faster than you can effectively engage your adversary. The adversary might be a spreadsheet, a concern, or a problem. Your adversary could be a death or a loss. You never want to move faster than you can effectively maneuver or handle that adversary. When you pinpoint what it is that you are trying to accomplish, you provide an overwhelming amount of dominating force in order to achieve it.

Apple trees only make apples.

They do not make peaches, they don't make plums, and they don't make figs. Apple trees only make apples because they are in the business of making apples. That's what apple trees do best. The same thing is true when you take your focus, balance, endurance, and flexibility and then spread them over a wide area: you will not be as effective. When you magnify your focus to a specific objective, it becomes much more effective. In physics, a dynamic force is described as the amount of acceleration of velocity needed to move an object. **What object do you need to move? How dynamic are you in moving that object? Are your actions creating dynamic force?**

Keep in mind that you are what you think. **What thoughts dominate your mind? Are your thoughts coming from a mindset of scarcity, or are your thoughts empowering you to win?**

Properly applied focus will view problems as opportunities. Focus applied in this way allows you to apply all your talents in overcoming anything that gets in your way. Without focus, your talents will not be utilized, and the problems remain problems. Focus is about

YES/NO
Describe

Detail

List

Confirm

YES/NO
Describe

Detail

List

Confirm

singleness—singleness of action and singleness of purpose.

I was reading the Bible recently, and every time it mentioned the word *man*, I substituted my name. Reading it that way for thirty days changed my focus because it showed me where I was supposed to be. I read it with singleness of purpose. Some people refer to singleness of purpose as "being in the zone," and when they're in the zone, things seem to happen in slow motion. It seems like time slows down only because you have deafened the other senses.

When you are focused, it gives you an opportunity to see things that other people don't see. Others don't fail to see because something is not there but because they're scattered and unfocused.

Remember the mission I shared earlier, the one with the gas truck parked in a Walmart parking lot? That story is a great example of what I'm talking about. We ran out of gas in Houston, and the Texas Department of Transportation sent several gas trucks to help people get gas and get them further down the road. One of the gas trucks was in the middle of a Walmart parking lot, and several cars had blocked it from moving. People were mad because they were running out of gas, and it was becoming a situation that could easily turn into a riot. Another trooper and I were ordered to secure the truck and get it back on the highway. I remember thinking to myself, "How are just two men going to go to this parking lot filled with a couple hundred people and move a gas truck?"

But we did it. We did it through focus.

All of those people were unfocused, scattered, and disoriented. They could have stopped us—they had the numbers, but we had the focus. People talk about being in the flow, or in the zone, and that's what happened that day. One-hundred percent of our balance, endurance, and flexibility had the opportunity to be focused in on a single effort.

Millenia ago, when they first begin shaping steel into swords, the steel had to be tempered. To do that, the blacksmith had to heat the metal until it glowed red, then pound it with his hammer, thus bundling the metal together. This process was repeated many times until the sword was strong. When we have singleness of focus, we temper ourselves so that we will have strength when we need it.

Deciding what to do, or not do, is only difficult when the goal or purpose is cluttered or undefined . When something isn't defined, it lacks clarity and focus.

The mandate for focus is purpose. I know that I want to be a great father;

YES/NO

Describe

Detail

List

Confirm

YES/NO
Describe

Detail

List

Confirm

that's my clearly defined goal. Let's say that someone said to me, "Hey, man, let's go hang out and smoke some dope." Now, my purpose is clear. I want to be a great father. Will smoking dope take away from that goal, or will it add value to the pursuit of that goal? Because my goal, my purpose, is clear, I have no difficulty in saying no to the invitation to smoke dope.

Conversely, if someone asked whether I'd like to read together, I would accept because it adds value to the pursuit of my goal.

Notes

_____

_____

_____

_____

_____

_____

_____

_____

_____

_____

_____

_____

_____

_____

_____

_____

_____

_____

_____

_____

_____

_____

_____

_____

_____

_____

_____

_____

_____

_____

_____

_____

_____

_____

_____

_____

_____

_____

_____

_____

_____

_____

_____

_____

_____

_____

_____

_____

CHAPTER 7

STRENGTH

We have discussed the need for balance, psychological endurance and flexibility, as well as focus. These are all individual components that must be brought together to work in harmony toward a specific outcome. The ability to do that is your strength. Strength, in this context, is the control you exercise over those individual components. Possessing them is important, but you must be able to combine them harmoniously in order to create a warrior mindset.

Consider your body and the way in which you are made. There are atoms, which combine to form molecules. Molecules are what make up cells, cells become tissue and, finally, organs. Organs then combine into systems and give you life.

YES/NO
Describe

Detail

List

Confirm

YES/NO
Describe

Detail

List

Confirm

There are several different components that make up your body, and any of those components by themselves will not give you life. However, bring them all together to work in a harmonious way, and you have a body that is alive and able to do amazing things.

This is how it works when you attain balance, endurance, flexibility, and focus and then combine them in a coordinated way. Together they bring life to whatever endeavor you are engaged in and make it possible to do amazing things. If you are weak in any area of your life, these things combined will make you stronger.

Men have a definition of strength that is often aligned with the definition they were given. Regardless of socioeconomic status or where they lived—suburbs, rural, or inner city—a child often models strength from their dad or friends or teammates in high school or college. At some point, we've got to recalibrate to see if what we are believing is true. Have you been sold a lie? Are you believing a lie, or is what you believe about the strong man and what strength is true?

Let's start by defining the truth about strength and the difference between strength and power. Power is the application of specialized knowledge and or abilities for the purpose of explosive effort that makes motion, while strength is a capacity of volume we can sustain.

An example of strength is an offensive lineman that can squat or deadlift 1,000 pounds. The balance of his body structure, the endurance of his muscle system, and the flexibility of his joints all focused and in concert give him the capacity to sustain the volume of the weight. Thus, the athlete is strong.

An example of power can be attributed to a basketball player. Though he cannot sustain the volume the football player could in the previous example of strength, he can jump from the free throw line to dunk a basketball. Though the basketball player is not as strong, he is more powerful in the arena of jumping. His ability to transform stillness into motion shows us how powerful his legs are.

Often strength and power are confused or thought of as the same thing. It's important to note they are not as we discuss the application of strength in our lives. The staple of strength is its capacity to withstand the volume of pressures that attack the core components of balance, endurance, flexibility, and focus to accomplish a purpose. *Capacity* and *volume* are key words in this definition. Capacity is defined as the maximum amount a thing can contain. Volume

YES/NO
Describe

Detail

List

Confirm

YES/NO
Describe

Detail

List

Confirm

measures the amount of space a thing occupies. These words identify strength as the maximum amount of resilience one can endure while occupying a space that delivers a purpose or desired effect.

Once I identified strength in this manner, I learned that aggressive action did not always secure effective action. As I matured and implemented this definition of strength, I lost some of my ego as I began to measure strength not by what the facts said or how I appeared but rather what the truth was and how it related to me obtaining a purpose or ending I designated as primary.

Kalief Browder was a 16-year-old boy accused of stealing a backpack. Browder would later be dismissed of the charges and found not guilty. The result of the accusation and his inability to pay a $3,000 bond or $950 bail was a three-year, one-thousand-day incarceration in one of the most dangerous prisons in America, Rikers Island. Seven hundred of those days were in solitary confinement. During Browder's time in Rikers Island, he was tortured, starved, and beaten by both inmates and correctional officers. Video accounts and interviews of his imprisonment record guards pepper spraying Browder in the mouth, hitting him in his ribs, snapping his back over metal rails, and slamming his face into concrete walls. The beatings from other inmates—jumpings—were frequent. Rikers was known for the fights, stabbings, slashings, and the acts of setting people on fire as they slept. Investigations of Rikers also identified it was common place for feces to be left on the walls for days while mice and spoiled milk saturated the floor.

During Browder's stay at Rikers, he had over thirty court dates. During many of these court dates, he had the opportunity to accept a plea bargain deal and be allowed to go home. In an interview, when asked why he didn't take the deal, he stated, "I didn't do it. You're not gonna make me say I did something just so I can go home." Browder later was freed from Rikers. Soon after being freed and found not guilty, he committed suicide. The post-traumatic effect of the one thousand days of incarnation inside the concentration camp of Rikers proved too much for him to bear.

I tell this story to give an illustration of strength, the maximum amount of resilience one can endure while occupying a space that delivers a purpose or desired effect. His purpose was to prove his innocence and stay true to himself. I believe this is a true testament of strength.

YES/NO
Describe

Detail

List

Confirm

YES/NO
Describe

Detail

List

Confirm

On Christmas Day 2017, Acorine Adams, president of Society's Angels allowed allowed me to serve alongside her as vice president of the nonprofit organization that serves food to children and families in need. We had served over eighty thousand meals to children during the summer food program within a three-year period and began adopting and serving a community in Dallas. Christmas Day was chosen by the president because no shelters served food on the actual day of Christmas. After serving on Christmas, we partnered with another nonprofit organization and served food and clothing every third Saturday of the month. We began to really make an impact. We started serving four hundred to five hundred people per programming.

Willie Thomas, the first Black person to work in the Commercial Vehicle Enforcement (CVE) section of the Texas Highway Patrol, passed away in February 2018. Willie served as my recruit school counselor and as a mentor as I worked with the CVE section. The day of his funeral marked the third commitment of the feeding and clothing program I had initiated. Knowing the great man Willie was and based on conversations he and I had about efforts in the community, I chose to be present at the feed and clothing program rather than attend the funeral. I believed and still believe that a true testament to his life is to live as he lived. Willie would give you the shirt off his back, and every time you saw him, he had a smile on his face. When he laughed, he roared. Willie stood six-foot-five and wasn't a small man. He was strong as an ox, and if he grabbed you, you knew you had been grabbed. I used to hate shaking his hand.

Just before starting the program that day, I received a text. The text read, "Where are you?" I responded, "I'm at my feeding and clothing program." The reply said, "Are you for real?" Many of the brothers I worked with didn't agree with me working at the feeding instead of attending the funeral. Some didn't think I properly paid my respects, and some didn't think I was being a good team player.

I relate this decision to strength. My relationship with Willie and the manner in which I grieved his passing were a personal endeavor. No different than choosing to cry or not cry at a funeral, neither identifies who is grieving the most. Based on my convictions, passions, and purpose, I decided to live that day the way he lived most of his days: in service. We served over five hundred people that

YES/NO

Describe

Detail

List

Confirm

YES/NO

Describe

Detail

List

Confirm

day. My ability to bear the weight of ridicule and occupy the space where others didn't or couldn't understand my actions or even like me or my actions as a person was related to my balance, endurance, flexibility, and focus. True strength is always related to purpose. Strength unrelated to purpose creates injury, abuse, and waste.

What's your focus?

Notes

CHAPTER 8

THE PRINCIPLE OF SEEDS AND FRUIT

No matter where you are in life, God can do big things in you and through you. In order to fully live out your purpose, it is important to understand the principle of seeds and fruit. The principle of the seed states that everything that a seed is to be is trapped inside of it and awaiting the proper environment for it to be revealed. Inside every seed is the genetic blue print for an entire forest of the fruit the seed carries. Likewise, you are pregnant with the fruit of your purpose. You are carrying precious cargo and your goal in life is to die empty, leaving it all on the field of life.

Who Am I?

This a question of identity. Identity is the concept of who you are. If you place a

YES/NO

Describe

Detail

List

Confirm

YES/NO
Describe

Detail

List

Confirm

diamond worth 10 Billion dollars inside a mountain of cow manure, does the diamond lose its value? No!!!! The cow manure becomes valuable. No different than you. Your value doesn't change because you're not in the place your purpose designates for you. However, until you recognize your value you will treat yourself and everything around you with the value you place on yourself. You are created in the image of God.

What is the identity of God?

Regardless what your concept is of God, and regardless of your understanding of God, there are two names given to God that define the identity of God. Those two characteristics are *omnipotent* and *omnipresent*. Omnipotence means God is all-powerful. Omnipresence means that God is everywhere at the same time, always being present and in all places at all times. This speaks to balance. It is impossible to be balanced without being present.

Omnipotent can also be seen and pronounced as omni-potential. It's broken down into two words, omni and potential. This means "always potent."

How does this impact your daily life?

Potent is the word for something strong, and it speaks directly to the seeds and fruit in your life.

God is always potent.

A seed is the same way. A seed is the very definition of potent potential awaiting the right environment to produce its fruit.

When you hold a seed in your hand, the fact is, it's a seed. It's a container. But what is a seed?

A seed may appear as a small thing.

What we see on the outside is the hard shell that contains the potency of what is inside. The hard shell we identify as the seed is the container that transports the essence and potency of the seed from one place to another.

The shell serves to protect the integrity of the seed.

The outside of the seed is the character or the piece that holds that integrity of the seeds purpose safe so that when it is planted in its proper environment, it has all the essential necessities it needs to become itself. Likewise, our character and integrity (the alignment with our divine purpose) keep the potency of our gifts safe until we find the place we are to use them and provide the world our fruits.

What that teaches us is that the future of a thing is inside itself; the future of you, the future of the things you have yet to become or yet to do are inside you. When

YES/NO

Describe

Detail

List

Confirm

YES/NO
Describe

Detail

List

Confirm

God made man by blowing himself into dirt, he filled use with the seeds of potential.

The fact is, that the seed is just a seed.

The fact is that it's just a small shell. The truth is that the seed is a tree.

But not only is this seed a tree, it's a tree that bears fruit.

Not only is the seed a tree that bears fruit. The seed is a tree that will bear fruit that will bear additional seeds.

Those seeds will bear other trees that bears fruit and so on and so on. The truth is that when you're holding this seed, you're holding a tree.

The bigger truth is you're holding a forest.

The facts refer to the present state of a thing. Truth is the reality of a thing. The Truth states that when you hold a seed in your hand you are holding a forest.

That is the principle of seeding.

Like the seed that bears fruit. Our father bears us as seeds. Those seeds are deposited into our mother's womb and nurtured until we are ready to be born into the world. You are a forest awaiting to be cultivated. Your dreams and visions are your compasses. The blueprint to your purpose is inside you. External factors will mold you, but the essence of your greatness was birthed with you. Stop looking to find yourself in other things. Listen to the spirit given to you by your creator. It speaks from inside you. You are an original, you have a gift that no one else can provide the world.

When you see the truth this way, you can see how God's forest for your life is so much bigger than you can possibly imagine.

Inside every seed is a forest waiting to grow. Every seed is awaiting the proper environment to grow. If you put a seed on a countertop or a tile floor, that seed lies dormant. That potential lies dormant. It's dormant not because the seed is impotent but because the seed hasn't been placed in the right environment.

If the seed is sitting on a tile floor within a home that's air conditioned in the summer and heated in the winter, the seed is very, very comfortable, but it lies dormant. When it's dormant, it doesn't grow.

The Danger of the Comfort Zone

In order for that seed to release its potency, it must first be drowned or submerged. It must be put in dirt and covered in darkness or fully submerged in water.

Part of the process of our potential growing and being realized is the process of being buried and overwhelmed. What we do in the dark is what people see later

YES/NO
Describe

Detail

List

Confirm

Detail

List

Confirm

in the light. **How do you cultivate yourself when no one is looking?**

Most people wear masks. Rather than face themselves with the intent to BECOME.......

As a seed is covered, natural pressure from the earth is applied. When that pressure is applied, the outside coating of the seed and the integrity of the seed is challenged.

You've experienced this in your life. You've experienced the pressure, felt suffocated, and likely wondered if you'd ever see out of the darkness. That process of growth is necessary. Every seed must face the pressure.

When a seed opens, its potential oozes out into the ground in a process called germination. When a seed begins to germinate you can see the roots start to sprout. The roots begin to sprout first, going downward, because in order to build anything of substance, the foundation must be created first.

In today's time of social media this is over looked and often lost. A baby develops inside its mother, the seed required to make life resides inside the father, visions and dreams are first witnessed inside the imagination. Birthing purpose and life must first be done in the dark. Not because its hiding but because life is precious and must be protected against the dangers of the world.

A seed does not first become what it's supposed to be. It first secures itself by extending its integrity. The pressure doesn't break the integrity of the seed, it adds to it. The pressure of the earth integrates the seed with the soil. The integrity of the seed becomes strongly fixed in its new environment.

On the tile floor, the seed had no reason to germinate, and had no reason to secure itself, so the seed is pushed and rolled from one place to another. In the proper environment with pressure applied to it properly, the seed will find its foundation.

Grow Where You're Planted

"Grow where you're planted" is a phrase we've all heard before.

Oftentimes people say, "If I was there, I would have done this." Or "If I was somewhere else, life would be better," or "If I had that life or opportunity, I would be happy."

Grow where you're planted. If you need something to happen in order to be happy, you will never be happy. The strengthening process begins in the environment you stand in. Happiness doesn't come from the outside; happiness comes

YES/NO

Describe

Detail

List

Confirm

YES/NO
Describe

Detail

List

Confirm

from inside. You can be content where you are and still desire to be better.

You can be happy with yourself and desire to be more.

The seed that grows into the mighty oak must first germinate and become rooted in the ground where it sits. The idea of growing where you are planted is rooted in the idea of growing strong in the environment you presently stand so that you may be prepared for the environments to come. You BECOME not in spite of but because of your experiences.

There will always be the lumberjacks in your life ready with an axe to cut down your forest of potential before it blooms.

Even though you have potential and purpose, you may not be able to live it or become it until you've gained certain experiences. Being aware of something is not the same as having the intelligence to carry it out. Intelligence here is defined as the ability to carry out or create an action. A great example is the story of a police officer in Irving, Texas. A robber held a woman hostage after she left a check-cashing business. The robber held a weapon to the victim's throat and threated to kill her and attempted to hide behind the victim. Everyone that witnessed the situation had the awareness of understanding that something needed to be done, but an Irving police officer had the physical intelligence to take a shot that killed the suspect while leaving the victim safe.

The officer made that shot after thousands of hours on the range. Awareness translates to intelligence, the active ability to carry out an ability after diligence.

Understand your potential and purpose and move in the direction of your dreams.

Often your dreams move to the speed and degree for which you are prepared. When you are denied what you think is rightfully yours, find the part of yourself that needs to grow.

Find what part of yourself is missing.

Let that be your focus. Sometimes God will protect the thing you want from you because you're not ready for what you want.

If you stay focused on the right things and work hard, everything that is yours will be yours. If you do not, it won't.

Focus on the seed of potential planted within you and take action to prepare for the harvest to come. After your seed is put in its proper environment and pressure is applied to it, you become secure because your seed becomes rooted. Without the stress of pressure, a seed cannot germinate and secure roots. Without roots a seed cannot grow.

YES/NO
Describe

Detail

List

Confirm

YES/NO
Describe

Detail

List

Confirm

When a seed of potential is securing itself and rooting itself under pressure, it is also gathering the nutrients it needs in order to grow into its potential.

Going through a process and not receiving the nutrients of knowledge taught from the experience is called failure. What if failure is just a step in the process?

Failure is the nutrient given to use by our environment. When something doesn't go your way, don't pout or become bitter, become **BETTER**.

Instead of allowing failure the means to consume you allow it to grow you by answering the questions of: **"How can I strengthen myself?" "What about me was not ready for this?"** Root yourself and become stronger. Prepare yourself. Create the opportunity for a different outcome the next time you're put in the same situation.

Don't become a slave to what you want. Use the process of obtaining the components of what you want as a path for growth. By working on the components of strength, by gathering and becoming more balanced and having more endurance, flexibility, and focus, you can become stronger in any area of your life you decide you want to exert more strength in. This is a principle of truth.

When God wanted to make plants, he spoke to the ground. When God made fish, he spoke to the water. When God wanted to make stars, he spoke to the firmament. When God wanted to make man, he spoke to himself.

Think about that. When God made man, he spoke to himself.

The word father originally did not have a male female designation. The word father originally translates to mean source, provider, sustainer. **Who is your father? Where are you sourced?** Being created in the image of God means to be created with his attributes. No different than a child born with the genetic attributes of their parents. The DNA of the parents creates the image of the child. What DNA does our father (God) pass to us his children created in his image?

The principle of seeding is important because it speaks to answering the questions of self-image.

We describe God as omnipotent. Omnipotent translates to always having potential.

After creating the sky, ocean, every plant, animal, countless earths, galaxies, stars, and more God has the potential to create more because he is always pregnant with more. And so are we.

Our potential is limitless.

YES/NO
Describe

Detail

List

Confirm

YES/NO
Describe

Detail

List

Confirm

Often the enemy of our future success is the present success we have achieved. As long as we're still standing, there is more inside of us to be given to the world. The successes we achieve become the fruit that we bare to the world. The baring of good fruit creates our leadership. Leadership is more about self-discovery than it is leading others. When we find our purpose/gift we find our personal leadership. Followers are attracted to the gift of good fruit.

The cultivating of ourselves creates our leadership. Leadership is not measured by the amount of people that follow you, for manipulation can also cause people to follow you. Our leadership begins the moment we plant ourselves in fertile ground and put ourselves in an environment of personal growth. The process of gathering our footing, and become rooted in our thought's beliefs, and actions grants us integrity. We must grow in the darkness where we are planted first. The growth we experience in the dark is what people see in the light.

We are going to break the surface, and people will realize and say, "There's a tree there! There's a tree there, there's an apple tree there, there's a mango tree there!" But that tree has been there for years and years and years, cultivating itself and preparing itself to be seen. You think you're seeing a baby tree, but this tree has been in existence for years and years. The tree grows first underground, then above ground, and finally you see fruit hanging from it.

You're attracted to the fruit that the tree is bearing. It's the same for our leaders. Our leadership is not going out and gathering people by saying, "Follow me!" Our leadership is about bearing righteousness and baring sweet fruit. As we bear that fruit, followers come not because of who we are but because of the fruit that we produce.

My daughter and I went to an open mic night where we both performed poetry. It was a beautiful night. My daughter found one of her skill sets as a poet and more as an orator.

After she performed and recited her poem, she went to the restroom, came back, and said, "Dad, Dad, all these women wanted to talk with me!" My daughter was only fifteen years old, women in their early twenties and mid-twenties come to her and said that they looked up to her. She was surprised and asking, "How can they look up to me? I'm only fifteen years old!"

What I explained to her that night, and what she learned that night, is that

YES/NO

Describe

Detail

List

Confirm

YES/NO
Describe

Detail

List

Confirm

when you speak truth, it is just like turning on a light, and it will attract others.

Her ability to speak truthfully and cut herself open in front of others drew others to her regardless of age, sex, or mindset. It drew people to her because the fruit of truth is sweet and draws people near.

My daughter learned an aspect of leadership that night. She experienced the power of bearing righteous fruit. Through the vulnerable truthful sharing of her imperfection's others were drawn to her. Most people are not truthful because they don't want to be vulnerable.

They don't want others to see who they truly are or how they truly feel because they're scared, they're going to be hurt. It is impossible to be a leader—a true leader, a sustainable leader—and not be true to yourself. As women's rights leader Elizabeth Cady Stanton said, "Truth is the only solid ground to stand upon."

In truth, we stand on firm ground, which allows us to grow and bear sweet and righteous fruit. By finding our gift, we find our source of personal leadership. By finding our gift, we answer the question of **"What should we do? What should we not do?"** You find your identity, and you discover the forest and become it.

Notes

_____

_____

_____

_____

_____

_____

_____

_____

_____

_____

_____

_____

_____

_____

_____

_____

_____

_____

_____

_____

_____

_____

_____

CHAPTER 9

LEADERSHIP: WHAT ARE YOU BECOMING?

YES/NO

Describe

Detail

List

Confirm

As a young man, I decided that I wanted to be an athlete. It wasn't until later in life that I understood that I wanted to be a transformational leader. As an athlete, the decisions I had to make about smoking, drinking, and many other things were already made for me. I knew that I couldn't do those things and obtain my dreams. They would derail me. I didn't make those choices arbitrarily; I made them in order to refine myself.

Those decisions were made to realize my gift and in order to bear the fruit of my vision.

While attending a family reunion in Detroit, I met a younger cousin that I had never met before. He was about to

YES/NO
Describe

Detail

List

Confirm

graduate from high school and was lost because he didn't know what his next move was. Other male family members told him he needed to cut his hair (he had dreadlocks) and do different things to be accepted by potential employers.

I disagreed with that approach, and I could see the discontent created by his disconnect from our older male family members. I asked him, "What do you want to do? What makes your heart sing?" He said, "Cousin, I want to be a boxer, and I want to work in a bank." I was surprised and elated that he had such a clear desire and want. No one else knew what he wanted because no one had ever asked.

I said, "Well, let me suggest this approach. Walk into three banks and ask to speak to the branch manager of each bank. Tell them what your aspirations are and ask what would be required of you to meet those aspirations. Once you identify where you are presently and what you would need to do in order to reach your dream, then decide on what you are willing to do. If they require you to cut your hair or go to a specific school, decide on what you are willing to sacrifice for your dream. Make the decision to change based on your willingness to grow and obtain what you want not because you want to be accepted."

Decide your next action based on what you want to become. The questions of **"what am I doing"** and **"what am I becoming"** are two different vantage points. The idea of fulfilling potential and producing fruit is always a question of what you are becoming, what seeds you are planting, and what fruit will you bear.

Now the question is how do we differentiate our purpose from our ambitions?

That question is answered by assessing whether the fruit, the potential, and the gift that you want to produce betters the world. If what want we want betters either the world or the earth, what you have is a gift from the Creator given to you to share for the betterment of humanity.

If the fruit that you want only benefits you, for example the obtaining of a new car or a nice house, it's not a vision of purpose. That's personal drive. That's ambition. It's important to make that distinction because we all have things we want. Ambition is not bad, but it must be separate, and we must understand the difference between an ambitious motive and an intent to grow something that's going to better the world of humanity and or grow your teams efforts.

By separating the two, we are allowed to always inspire instead of manipulate. Manipulation occurs when you put

YES/NO
Describe

Detail

List

Confirm

a man in the way or as the cause of an action. Manipulation means "man did."

Inspiration begins when you go inside to attract someone's spirit with inspiration. You inspire; you are in spirit.

As we go through this life, **how are we graded? How do we realize our own seed of potential?** If they're growing and they're growing properly, how are we measured? The facts say the older you are, the more you must be doing something right.

We often think that if we live to be one hundred years old, you had to be doing something right. The truth says that God doesn't measure our lives by chronological age but by productive or purposeful moments.

Would you rather be the guy that lives to be a thousand years old that sits in his home, measuring what he eats, living in fear, only doing fragments of things because he's scared that he's going to hurt himself or scared that he's not going to step outside those bounds? Or would you want to be the person who lives fewer than fifty years but every day is a purpose-filled moment?

Every day, every time he's breathing, he's adding value to himself and the world around him. He's not living in fear but in victory. That person leverages himself in all that he does.

The fact is that the world measures life by chronological order. The truth is God measures our life by the completion of our purpose. Remember, the facts refer to a present state of a thing, but the truth speaks to the reality of a thing. Your reality is that you are wonderfully and uniquely made. Your present state doesn't define you...... Your purpose, actions, and thoughts do!

In order to be a strong leader, you must protect your purpose. God measures our life by purpose-filled production. This requires action, and action often requires faith.

I don't believe it's possible to please God without faith. What is faith? Faith is the believing of things yet to be done. God is always full of potential. That is a description of faith.

God speaks to the material (components) of what he intends to create not to the product of his creation.

God spoke to the ground and made plants.

God spoke to the water and made fish.

God spoke to the gases and fermanet and made stars

God spoke to himself and made man!

YES/NO

Describe

Detail

List

Confirm

These are all acts of faith. The speaking to the present state of a thing with the intent to create its reality.

That's why God is excited about our potential. That is the fundamental understanding of the principle of seeding and fruiting.

You are here, and you were created for a purpose. All boys are seeds to become trees of fathers. All girls are created to mother. What does that mean? We look at the words *father* and *fathering* in the Hebrew context. Neither word *Abba* in Hebrew or *Pata* in the Greek has a sexual designation.

It was a description that meant source, sustainer, provider, teacher, the foundation, protector, and provider. When a boy becomes a man, he becomes a father, and he fathers in every environment that he walks into. Fathering is not about the bearing of children. Fathering and mothering is about the condition that you create by your presence. As a mother, it is being able to nourish, incubating growth, nourishing growth in every environment you encounter.

These components are the aspects of the seed full of potential. This is potency encapsulated, waiting for the proper atmosphere to grow. As we grow, we create new environments for us to grow in.

We are in a constant state of growing. We are the forest and the seed. The forest are the things that we leave behind. The acts and the deeds that we have allowed to grow, the fruit, is what we're bearing for people to see. And the seed is a new place that we're going into. The only difference between a forest and a garden is how we organize it. Take a second to look and think back.

One, have you left gardens or a forest on your trail?

Two, where does your forest lead?

Three, what fruit are you bearing currently?

The future is the present we give ourselves in this day. The things we did yesterday allow us to be where we are today. The things we do today create the opportunities that we have tomorrow. **What present are you giving yourself?** Both failure and success are measurable. Neither is a surprise. If you're a young man or woman that is smoking cigarettes at twelve or thirteen years old, I can tell you your future. You can be prophesied to. Your lungs are going to give out on you.

If you're drinking alcohol on a regular basis when you're fifteen years old, I can tell you your liver is not going to withstand that. The future is encoded in your

YES/NO

Describe

Detail

List

Confirm

Y E S / N O
Describe

Detail

List

Confirm

action. Success can be measured. Failure can be measured. If I have accurate, detailed descriptions of what you do on a daily basis, in a week's time, in a month's time, I can tell you what you will be in a year, two years, three years from now. **What fruit are you bearing?** It's not a secret. The principle of the seed, the principle of fruit. You must bury yourself. You must work in the dark. You must allow pressure to be placed on you. You must allow your integrity to be firmly rooted in the ground that you stand on and not be pushed away or broken. You must not allow the seeds of your excuses derail your potential.

EXCUSES

"Excuses are tools of the weak and incompetent, used to build monuments of nothingness, those who use them, seldom amount to anything but excuses"
—*Author Unknown*

Definition:

Incompetent – *inadequate to or unsuitable for particular purpose, lacking the qualities needed for effective action, unable to function properly*

Monuments – *a building, statue, etc. that honors a person or event also attributed to a character of a thing*

Have you created gardens, or have you created forests?

When you look back, **where does your forest lead?**

What are you doing on a regular basis, a consistent basis? This will determine the fruit that you will bear. **If you don't like the fruit that you're bearing, what actions can you change to bear the fruit that you wish to bear?**

The fruit we produce results in the seeds we plant. **Are you consistently in unity or conflict? Are you reaping ripe or spoiled harvest?** The justification of our actions are always determined by the results of our action rather than our ability to argue why we are right.

YES/NO

Describe

Detail

List

Confirm

Notes

_____

_____

_____

_____

_____

_____

_____

_____

_____

_____

_____

_____

_____

_____

_____

_____

_____

_____

_____

_____

_____

_____

_____

_____

_____

_____

CHAPTER 10

WHAT'S YOUR ORIGIN STORY?

YES/NO
Describe

Detail

List

Confirm

According to Greek mythology, a phoenix is a long-lived bird that perishes and then is regenerated back to life from the ashes of its own death. The pattern is repeated, and so the phoenix never dies.

Because the phoenix is associated with the sun, a phoenix obtains new life by rising from the ashes of its predecessor. According to mythical stories, the phoenix dies in the flames and combustion of the sun and decomposes before being born again in all its glory and splendor. In the historical record, the phoenix symbolizes renewal in general and its symbolic reference.

In effect, the phoenix ends up destroying itself. The thing that the phoenix

YES/NO
Describe

Detail

List

Confirm

struggles with is maintaining balance so that it doesn't become so hot that it incinerates everything that it cares about and itself in the process. But every time the phoenix fails, it comes back, so this is not a situation where it can lose because of its fear of not coming back; it is a fear of its inability to maintain control of its God given powers and gifts. Our gifts are always tested. They become our curses when there not aligned with our purpose.

All warriors walk a path. That path is illustrated by a code. What is your code? A warrior consistently battles for balance. The balance of measuring if aggressive action is effective action. The balance of understanding a hammer has two sides. One to hammer nails in and the other to take nails out. The warrior walks with both sword and shield in tow. The text on the shield, "Pray as I Will Die Tomorrow." Pray as though this is your last prayer, pray as this is the last time you'd be able to go before God before to be judged and held accountable.

The text on the sword, "Live as I Will Never Die!" **If there was no such thing as failure, what would you do? How would you fight? If you knew that you would never get tired and you would never get hurt, how would you fight?** The sword and the shield are the weapons of the warrior. They are the balance the phoenix aspires to maintain. I'm going to pray with all humility as though I would die. I'm going to make repentance. I'm going to love as if I will not have an opportunity to love again. But at the same time, I will be so ferocious in my fight and in my conviction, I will fight as though I will never die.

Origin Stories

Every superhero has an origin story.

An origin story is an account or back-story revealing how a character gained its super powers and /or the circumstances under which they became superheroes or supervillain.

Our origin stories are the experience that birth our perceptions of the world. Our origin stories are places we find ourselves planted and grow most from.

What origin story fuels you?

What origin story fails you?

Superhero's are defined by their super-natural powers. The term *Supernatural* is defined as the manifestation of events attributed to some force beyond scientific understanding or the law of nature. The characteristics of the human spirit such as whearwithal, empathy, love, etc are forces beyond scientic understanding or the laws of nature. True supernatural powers are not some esoteric gifting

YES/NO

Describe

Detail

List

Confirm

YES/NO
Describe

Detail

List

Confirm

given to a select few humans. Our super-natural power is the gift of free will to use the imeasurables of the human spirit.

What is your superpower?

How many supernatural things have you done?

How many times have you done or been a part of something that could not be explained? How many times have you been a superhero? Rather how many times have you used your natural gifts to benefit others? One of my personal superpowers is resiliency. I have been in several situations where I walked beside death or failed, yet it didn't stop me. It is because of those experiences that I am able to be resilient today and am able to see myself as an individual who can con-tinue on in the face of adversity.

In 2011, I arrested a man traveling home with his wife. He and his wife had just left a house party, and he was intoxi-cated. After arresting him, I sat him in the front seat of my patrol car. A sergeant was with me that night. As I sat in the front seat inputting information into the computer, the sergeant was getting some paperwork out of the backseat. We sat parked on the side of the highway. Suddenly, **BAM-MMM!!!!** Another intoxicated driver hit us from behind traveling at a speed faster than seventy miles per hour.

The speed was never determined because he never touched his brakes. No skid marks were left in order to calculate the driver's speed at the time of impact. He plowed straight through us; the Sergeant was knocked unconscious, and everyone else was injured. I couldn't call for help using the radio because the vehicle hit us so hard that the radio was dislocated and now sat under the hood beside the engine block. We survived that night because I found a way to find my wits and push through the stress of the incident. That night left permanent damage and memories.

The sergeant working with me that night would die on the operation table seven times and resurrect from the dead seven times. He would also suffer from multiple injuries and lives with a drop foot for the rest of his career. I would suffer nerve damage and whiplash.

It was supernatural that everyone in the crash survived. It was supernatural that the sergeant would hold on to his life when all indications said he wouldn't make it. It was supernatural that after eight months I would return to work and through the superpower of resiliency be able to train and prepare for the first ever Special Response Team 1, a team within the Special Operation Division of the

YES/NO

Describe

Detail

List

Confirm

YES/NO
Describe

Detail

List

Confirm

Texas Rangers. There are superheroes among us. There might be one sitting in your seat.

There might be someone who has been through something so traumatic that it seemed impossible they'd survive, and there are others who have helped people through those moments. Maybe you're the survivor. Or maybe you're the one who helps others.

What makes us superheroes?

What gives us the opportunity to be a superhero?

God, our Creator, is the source that pours into us and designs us to be a resource for the betterment of humanity. Our purpose on Earth is related to our gifts, or as I like to call them, superpowers. A gift is just a gift wrapped up tight until you unwrap it. If you have a gift, the only way to make it a superpower is to unwrap it, deploy it, use it. The gift isn't meant to just sit dormant.

This unswervingly relates to the idea of an origin story. Origin stories are unique, and of course both superheroes and supervillains have them. The only difference between the superhero and a supervillain is their perspective of love. That's it. They both go through a challenge. They both go through ordeals that challenge their belief system, challenge their character, and they have found some sort of integrity.

Oftentimes when we talk about integrity, we think of it positively. However, you can have an ill-placed sense of integrity. If you look at the stories of super criminals, their stories tell the tale of elaborate events, how they evaded law enforcement for years and years and years. Their integrity is identified with the alignment of their thoughts, actions, and words. Their integrity and commitment make them powerful in their own right.

The difference between a superhero and a supervillain is identical to the difference between a wolf and sheepdog. They differ because of their perspectives on their origin story. One is manifested in love and the other hate. With that understanding, we must define the difference between love and hate. Oftentimes people think love and hate are opposite, but that's not true. Love and hate are kindred spirits. The opposite of both love and hate is indifference. You cannot hate something you did not first love. Hate is the unfulfilled, unrealized expectation of love. Hate is a version of love. Hate is the undefined, unreliable expectation of love. Hate is impotent love.

Now again, why is that important?

YES/NO

Describe

Detail

List

Confirm

YES/NO
Describe

Detail

List

Confirm

Because hate stems from impulses; hate fuels sickness and death in the body. **How does hate have this power? How can hate be so strong that it manifests sickness and death, that it can manifest cancer, that it can manifest suicide, that it can manifest murder? How is hate so strong?**

The supervillain's power is created by its tragedy and derives from its hate. It is defined from an unfulfilled, unrealized expectation or impulse of love. The hate that fills the supervillain is seeded in impotence. Impotency fuels sickness and death just as omnipotence fuels life. How does hate fuel these things? The answer is when we define God, we define the great architect of the seen and the unseen universe by two characteristics: omnipresent and omnipotent.

The very definition of God is always having potential, always having more. Therefore, hate being a product of impotency describes the nature of something opposite of God. Going back to the superhero versus supervillain, they're both the same person, no different than the wolf and the sheepdog. What categorizes them as a superhero or a supervillain is the perspective of love. Their outlook on love in relationship to their test gives them the perspective in describing their testimony.

The danger of the supervillain is that they, too, can manifest events attributed by supernatural forces. That is the power of hate. Being a villain or hero, a sheepdog or wolf, is a matter of choice. I have met both in my lifetime. It is my experience in tactical combat, law enforcement, and even in coaching leaders that has brought this collection of words to you today. It is not just my experience with the leaders or criminals or the lawbreakers or the law enforcers, for I have seen one be the other.

When wearing body armor—as a police officer wears a bulletproof vest during his shift or military personnel wear Kevlar during war—we are physically protected but only on part of our body. Body armor physically effects the person wearing it. It's not always comfortable. Body armor is worn close to the skin, and it rubs and irritates your skin, especially when it's hot outside. Though the body armor protection protects you from bullets and harm from the outside, the very thing that protects you from all the bullets and all the outside influences makes your skin tender on the inside, and it makes you vulnerable.

Oftentimes when you see superheroes, they are strong on the outside, deflecting, derailing things that come for them, but the things that tear them down

YES/NO
Describe

Detail

List

Confirm

are intimate things that stand between the body armor and their skin, like their spouses, their children, their family, things that stand in between them and their purpose. It's the things that require them to walk away from their purpose in exchange for a place of peace to rest and rejuvenate. As you wear body armor more and more and more, what happens is the effect doesn't change, the rub doesn't change. What does change is your sensitivity to the rub because you become calloused. This effect in the life of a sheepdog or superhero can be dangerous. Just because you don't feel something doesn't mean it doesn't have a negative effect.

As superheroes, we must be cognizant and aware of the things that we become callous to. We must also be aware that it is impossible to be a superhero at all times. You will become tired and exhausted. The relationships we have that are intimate to us, that are close to us, those relationships are the catalysts for support or can be the catalyst for destruction.

Proverbs 4:23 says to guard your heart. Superheroes must guard it from the bad guys but have discernment to let in the good.

We must guard our passions, convictions, purpose, and gifts by choosing our intimate relationships carefully. Our spouses and children must also understand and be aware that we will be Clark Kent when we come home and not to measure us against our greatness. Rather it must be understood that the power of our gifts elevates us; it doesn't lessen us.

Measuring our normalcy against our greatness creates division. It creates an atmosphere of proving, a continual state of proving that you are a superhero and that you deserve the title. When this happens, home is no longer a place of refuge; it is no longer a place of resourcing. When home is no longer a reservoir to come to and be filled, home can become a liability. It's impossible to consistently and effectively fight the world and not have a place to be replenished. Fighting the world and fighting at home is the equivalent of battling on two fronts. This is a recipe for failure, often ending in the walking away from one of the fights or neglecting one of the battles to find safety and comfort elsewhere.

Men and women of purpose who fight this fight and live on purpose pour much of themselves outside of themselves and into their dreams. The effect of doing everything tangible to build a vision is coming home drained. Every Superman needs a Lois Lane. Every Batman needs an Alford. Iron sharpens iron. We as

YES/NO
Describe

Detail

List

Confirm

YES/NO
Describe

Detail

List

Confirm

humans are communal and are built for community. Our net worth is only as strong as our network.

Every superhero needs someone to protect them from everything else when they are becoming strong again.

Depression is common among superheroes. They walk the world with a big stick, valued by the people they help and serve, edified by the world but torn down where they rest. Many of the CEOs and champions I have coached experience being seen as superheroes by the world only to be devalued at home. This is a tragedy; it rots them from the inside out. "You think you're special? If they only knew. You're nothing. You always try to do too much. Your dream is too big. You can't. You're not good enough." These are some of the statements I've heard personally and while coaching clients. These statements were made by people intimate to the heroes. This is where the seeds of depression can take root.

The hero receiving the negativity first becomes confused, later exhausted, and thirdly depressed. They ask themselves, "Why does the world see me as great, but my household, the place I need to feel valued, sees me as a failure?" Support systems are powerful. Even though you are a superhero, you need a support system.

Even though you're a superhero, you will be Clark Kent. Actually, you will be Clark Kent more often than you are Superman. Superman only pulls out his suit and abilities when something bad happens; Clark Kent goes to work every day. He has relationships with people. He writes the newspaper. In the process of knowing people as Clark Kent, he becomes reinvigorated and sensitive to an understanding of the people he has sworn to protect.

We are affected by time and change. What and or whoever controls your time and change controls your life. When a superhero's support system redirects their time spent on purpose and puts them through changes that negatively impact their spirit, the system is no longer a support system. It has become a hindering system. The depression formed within superheroes is brought on by the impotence of life and the failure to live a life on purpose. Depression is the result of one's purpose becoming a victim of someone else's priority. Whoever controls your time and change controls your future.

A superhero can be destroyed by its support system. What does your support system look like? A superhero can also be launched by his or her support system.

Christianity identifies good and evil as God and Satan. There is a battle

YES/NO
Describe

Detail

List

Confirm

YES/NO
Describe

Detail

List

Confirm

for your power, your purpose, and your mind. There's a battle for your offspring.

Through ignorance, we often think that there's a battle between God and Satan, but that's not actually true. The battle is for your life. You have free will, so which will you choose? There cannot be a battle between God and Satan because Satan was created by God. When he stepped out of his power, when he dislocated his power, he became demonic.

We all have the capacity to become angelic heroes or demonic destroyers, depending upon which path we choose. Not in the literal sense of becoming a supernatural being but in the literal sense of destroying the lives of those around you, including yours. We can become our own demons if we make the small compromises that lead us down a dark path.

Spiritually, God and Satan are supernatural beings, but we create our own on earth when we do things that cause us to give up our purpose and power.

So, the true definition of demonic, the true definition of a demon on earth, is anything that dislocates your power, anything that takes your power out of the position of purpose. This is important because there are many demons and demonic forces in our lives that we allow in our life. It's not some grand red guy in a red suit with horns and a pickaxe. It's a subtle thing that takes our power offline, and it becomes tragically demonic in our lives when it takes our purpose out of position. It's a slow fade.

What is purpose? Purpose is defined as the original intent of a thing.

As you realize your purpose, you will realize all that you are, and you'll see how all that you do was created specifically for you to do.

Ego and human nature can derail your purpose and relationships. Super-heroes are normal people fueled by their origin story to use their pain to fulfill their defined purpose.

How do we use our pain to fuel our power to fulfill our defined purpose?

The simple answer is by choosing to do so. However, many of us do not, choosing instead to dwell in pain until it drowns their purpose.

In that scenario, we build hedges of destruction around us or allow them to be built around us by others through their own actions. We teach people how to treat us through the actions we allow them to conduct with and around us.

How can all of this be circumvented? How do we move past these obstacles, whether real or perceived?

YES/NO
Describe

Detail

List

Confirm

YES/NO
Describe

Detail

List

Confirm

In all things seek understanding. Knowledge is obtained by seeking; understanding is a gift given through revelation. As we intentionally move on faith to learn more about ourselves and our defined purpose, God gifts us with his understanding. Seeking our purpose walks hand in hand with the seeking of God. The identification that you were created for a purpose identifies your relationship with the creator.

This relationship further identifies that you are not your experiences. The ego will attempt to devalue you and by identifying you as an experience of pain. This identification lessens who you are as well as lessens your Father (source, provider, manufacturer). Your experiences are merely the environments you travel through to strengthen you for your purpose. The heavier the load the greater the purpose.

Using your pain to power your purpose begins when you love yourself enough to walk away from everything that requires you to be and play small.

You were wonderfully and fearfully made......

BECOME

Notes

_____

_____

_____

_____

_____

_____

_____

_____

_____

_____

_____

_____

_____

_____

_____

_____

_____

_____

_____

_____

_____

_____

_____

_____

DEAR READER

Dear Reader,

What's your purpose? You may not have figured it out yet, but my hope is that this book is a guide for you along the way.

We are all a collection of stories—the stories we read, watch, experience, and more importantly, the stories we fear. More often than not, rather than living life, we pursue the avoidance of pain and failure. You cannot become your destiny if your sole purpose is the avoidance of pain. Pain will come, like it or not. The adolescent feels pain in his femur when he grows because of the pain of growing. Pain is a very active and real part of life, but it's temporary, flowing like the river rock tumbling down the bed of the river,

YES/NO
Describe

Detail

List

Confirm

YES/NO
Describe

Detail

List

Confirm

softening the stone's jagged edges. Each one of us is that stone flowing down the river, and every river, stream, stone, and path is different. You are unique. You will get bumped in life and tumble down the jagged rocks, but their sharp edges will make you better, even if it's adversity. Sometimes you'll be the one with the sharp edges.

What is the shape of the box you live in?

Is it a square, triangle, or rhombus? The boxes we live in are boxes tailored by our own hands. Boundaries, limitations, and fears are the pier and beams that frame the invisible fences where we reside. The moment I decided to walk away from all the things in my life that required me to be small is the moment I truly began to love and find myself.

There is a training method used when training dogs. The training method uses a shock collar to train for obedience. A collar with a remote electrical current is placed around the dog's neck. The shock collar has the ability to electronically shock the dog remotely.

One way to use the shock collar is to create an invisible fence. Markers are set on the boundary lines of a property. The collar is then programmed to remotely render an electronic shock after administering an audible warning once the collar approaches and passes boundary marks. The electronic shock is strong enough to cause discomfort but not strong enough to injure the dog.

After the dog becomes accustomed to hearing the audible sound and shock that follows, the dog no longer passes the mark. Thus, an invisible fence that creates an artificial boundary is created. The warning sound (warning signs of discomfort) becomes the markers for behavioral change.

This training method works on most dogs, especially when the trainer regulates the electronic current to match the pain tolerance of the dog being trained.

However, there is a special kind of dog that is rare and very valuable. This dog refuses to stop pushing forward in spite of the pain of the electronic current. The dog eventually pushes past the threshold of the remote and onto the other side of the invisible fence.

Ironically, once the dog does this, the sound of the audible tone identifies the approaching of a boundary and the painfulness of its re-entry. This makes the dog run away from the fence it resided in.

The stories we tell ourselves have the potential to recreate invisible fences laced in negative experiences that limit our growth.

YES/NO
Describe

Detail

List

Confirm

The components of strength you will read in this book are principles that you can apply to any area of your life where you want to become stronger.

At one point in my life, I wanted to live "outside the box," but as I continued to grow, I found no need for a box at all.

Over the past two-and-a-half decades I have experienced a multitude of successes and lessons, both deriving from experiences as a lifeguard, college football MVP, receiving an MBA, being a Jr. Olympic Championship coach, and serving as both a Texas Ranger Special Ops team member and international team builder / leadership coach.

The combination of my experiences inspires me to teach the ability to leverage leadership strengths to achieve extraordinary results. I have experienced both good and bad leaders. Quite frankly, I myself have been both a good and bad leader. Good leadership produces enhanced, productive decision-makers. This is why growing future leaders and building current leaders is so important to me.

Success without fulfillment is the ultimate failure. True leadership drives personal growth and fulfillment and maximizes potential. Contrary to popular belief, the obtaining of things, merits, and awards will not fulfill you. They are simply landmarks along the way.

While technology provides for understanding and driving improvements, research indicates the difference between average, good, and best-in-class performance is leadership and decision-making skills.

So, what is this thing we call leadership?

Leadership is leading, first yourself and then others. We can only produce what we are. We must first become valuable before we can build anything of value.

Great leadership is the capacity to influence by inspiration and motivate through the power of passion, conviction, and purpose. It requires courage. Each one of us must dig deep to find courage within.

Everyone has their turning-point moment.

In my TEDx Talk, I referred to the adversity and loneliness I faced as a youth, to the bullying that led me to become a fighter, and how when I was left alone in the house, how I learned to become a survivor. I cooked, scrounged for food, and laid in bed at night thinking of ways to survive. At school I was called names. Each one of these moments impacted

YES/NO
Describe

Detail

List

Confirm

how I evolved into the man I am today. If I hadn't had them, would I know how to fight? Would I instinctually react with a survivor mentality?

This fight mentality has served me well in my battles as a man. One of them came unexpectedly in my role as a state trooper on the side of the highway one night. It's a night forever etched in my memory where I was thrust into a situation that caused me to fight for my partner's life.

We were standing on the side of the road at 2:00 a.m.

Dallas has several well-known busy highways, and my sergeant, and I had just pulled over a suspicious intoxicated driver. No one wants to be standing on the side of the road on any busy highway at 2:00 a.m., but it's part of my job, and we do it. It's necessary. It's like a warrior on the battlefield. No one wants to be on the battlefield, but it's absolutely essential in order to stop the enemy. If you're not on the battlefield willing to fight, then the enemy advances. A true warrior knows when to enter and exit the battlefield.

On that night it was business as usual as my partner, DPS Sgt. David Cramer, and I began the process of determining whether the suspect we had pulled over was going to jail. David had been with the department for over a decade. Normally, officers don't ride together. When they do it's called check riding, and it is a form of quality control for inexperienced officers. Since we were both very experienced, it was more about just hanging out and working together. We were about to call it a night, and David had had a great idea.

"Let's just stop one more car before we take it in."

In any kind of law enforcement, we try never to say this. Why? The decision to do just one more call has been the beginning of many terrible stories. This wasn't an exception. It was not a great idea, but we couldn't have predicted what was to come.

We saw a car whiz by and took off after it, pulling him over.We parked our Chevrolet Tahoe with its emergency lights activated.

The car we pulled over had been speeding and swerving. We knew that he was driving too fast, and we pulled him over to take care of a speeding violation. However, the longer we talked to the driver, the more information he revealed that led to a different conclusion.

"We just came from a house party," he said. We continued talking to him and observed his actions, eyes, and words.

After a while, we knew that he had too much to drink. As he sat with his wife in the passenger seat beside him, we could

YES/NO
Describe

Detail

List

Confirm

YES/NO
Describe

Detail

List

Confirm

smell the alcohol on his breath, so we asked him to get out of the car to do a field sobriety test. He failed miserably.

Knowing that he was intoxicated, we handcuffed him and put him in the back of our car to begin processing him. His wife didn't seem drunk, but we wanted to take every precaution, so we had her make some calls to get a ride home while we finished the paperwork to take her husband to the precinct.

As we sat there working on the battlefield we work on every day, in an attempt to save lives, the unthinkable happened.

David, my sergeant, had been with the department for over thirty years, and had retired and come back. Maybe that's why he had said, "Just one more call": because he was so in love with his job and passionate about it. He didn't want to go in.

All the experience of those years couldn't prepare us for what happened next.

I was sitting in the driver's seat filling out the required paperwork with the arrested driver in the passenger seat, and he was not being problematic at all. He knew he had made a bad decision. Don was standing partially outside the patrol car, getting a form I needed to fill out, when a silver Mazda 626 veered off the roadway onto the shoulder and struck us at full driving speed.

What do you do when something unexpected happens?

You can stay down, or you can stand up and take charge. I was dazed, and I said, "Man, what just happened?" I looked over to the passenger, still hand-cuffed, who was yelling, "Somebody hit us, somebody hit us!" I turned to look, and all I could see in the backseat were headlights. The driver didn't even tap the breaks, and he had hit us so hard that he plowed right through us, launching our car forward into the car still containing our arrested driver's wife.

My first thought as I came out of the daze was, "Where is David?"

I looked around, and I didn't see him anywhere. I jumped out of the car to look for him, and when I found him, he was unconscious and bleeding out of every orifice I could see. I went into instant tri-age mode.

I had to make the decision to either help him or move on to the next person. I couldn't find a pulse, and he was bleeding everywhere. Immediately I went into fight mode. This was our battlefield. I was not going to let my partner die.

With the center console ripped out and with no cell phones, we had no means to get a hold of anyone. Then I remembered that the wife had her cell

YES/NO
Describe

Detail

List

Confirm

YES/NO
Describe

Detail

List

Confirm

phone. I ran to the car in front and took her phone. She was in so much shock from the impact that she could barely put the security code in to unlock it.

As I fought that day to save his life, my instincts kicked in. When it happens to you, let your warrior instinct take over and have faith that you will succeed.

If you look at the warrior tradition, you look to find a way to smile. It can save your life. In the movie *Gladiator*, when Maximus was talking to the emperor he said, "Death smiles at all of us; the only thing the warrior can do is smile back."

"You still look pretty," I told him as he woke up, stunned.

When I said that, it activated that moment, and he laughed despite the pain and the injuries.

Once I finished assessing everything, I looked over to the vehicle that hit us. I saw the guy who hit us sitting in his car and texting.

What would you do if the person responsible for nearly killing four people was sitting within arms' reach and texting? For me, I was filled with rage. I was out of the game in that moment because all I could think of was putting my hands on him. Luckily, when I went over to open the car door, it wouldn't budge. A semi came around the corner, and I felt it pass by, just inches from my back. It made me breathe again, and I realized that I needed to step away. I pulled the gentlemen that we arrested out of the car and laid him down next to David, and his wife came over. She asked, "Baby, are you okay?" That moment, the character of that man truly impacted me. Lying on the ground, handcuffed and having just been in an accident, he looked at his wife and said, "Don't worry about me, worry about him. Just make sure he doesn't die." He gestured at David.

The first man we handcuffed was worried about our safety and survival, not his.

Facedown in the mud, on the side of the road, this moment was a testament to his character. He rejected his wife's concern for himself to instead focus on the life of this unknown officer who had pulled him over with intent to arrest him.

When faced with a challenge, how will you react? Do you place blame, conceal the evidence, or risk your own life and reputation to save another?

Don died seven times that night.

One on the side of the road, and six more on the table as the hospital worked to save his life. Just like the proverb, fall down seven times, get up eight, he got back up. My injuries were less severe. It took eight months before I could return

YES/NO
Describe

Detail

List

Confirm

YES/NO
Describe

Detail

List

Confirm

to work, and when I found out about a new special response team created by the Texas Department of Public Safety and the Texas Rangers Special Ops Team, I decided to try out. The try out for that was six months from the date that I came back to work, and I was ready to get back in action. That became my motivation. I spent that six months training to get back to where I was before the accident but to also be better, to develop more resilience.

For David, it was two years to recover from the injuries we sustained that night. I dropped the charges of the man we pulled over, and when it came time to get the Purple Heart that David and I both received for our actions that night, it didn't come without a bitter taste.

As a warrior, you will stand up and do things that will never get you credit, things that are expected of you. If you always stand up for others, it may become expected of you. When we stood in front of our peers to receive the Purple Heart and the Star of Texas for that day on the side of the highway, I was doing my job. When I asked if I would receive any special commendations for saving the lives of everyone on the scene, I was told, "You didn't do anything special; you just did your job."

My life has been a series of moments that have been "in spite of." In spite of not having a father that was not addicted to drugs, in spite of going into foster care, in spite of awards and commendations, even in this moment of the accident, it was all about resiliency. Resilience is my superpower.

Everyone has a gift, and you have to find that gift and use it in everything you do. Mine is resiliency. **What about you?**

Here are two concepts that add value to me as I grow, and I hope they will also add value to you.

1. Deployment vs. Employment

Managers allocate resources, pens, paper, and budgets. Leaders grow people. Find and maximize your gifts. Deploy yourself. *Grow where you are planted.* I can't stress that enough. *Grow where you are planted.* Being awesome is a choice. You must lead yourself before you can lead others.

_____

_____

_____

_____

_____

_____

_____

_____

YES/NO
Describe

Detail

List

Confirm

YES/NO
Describe

Detail

List

Confirm

2.   Fear vs. Danger

Fear is not real; danger is. Fear is anticipating something that may or may not happen; therefore, fear is only real to the degree you empower it to make it real. Danger, on the other hand, is the understanding of a threat. We dampen fear with knowledge and defeat danger through preparation. When you're scared, it's time to grow strong, no different than the check engine light on your car signifies it's time for service. Grow your strength and capabilities by acquiring knowledge, prepare with understanding, and act!

_____

_____

_____

_____

_____

_____

_____

_____

_____

_____

_____

_____

WHAT'S NEXT?
30 DAY CHALLENGE

Exercises

The following exercises are tactical and designed to activate you to action.

1. Discover

Find and maximize your gifts. Deploy yourself. *Grow where you are planted*. I can't stress that enough. *Grow where you are planted*. Being awesome is a choice, and so is being an asset. Assets are the leaders who drive results. **What are the gifts inside of you that make you an asset to the people you work and live with and to everyone around you?**

_____

_____

_____

_____

_____

_____

2. Push

Every warrior understands the phrase "no pain, no gain." **In what areas of life do you know that you must push yourself more to succeed?** You must lead yourself before you can lead others. **List 3 areas below that you can focus on strengthening today.**

_____

_____

_____

_____

_____

_____

_____

3. S.M.A.R.T Goal

After listing 3 areas you desire to strengthen create a Specific, Measurable, Achievable, Relevant and Time Based goal "S.M.A,R.T. goal" to achieve your goals.

_____

_____

_____

_____

_____

_____

_____

Notes

_____

_____

_____

_____

_____

_____

_____

_____

_____

_____

_____

_____

_____

_____

_____

_____

_____

_____

_____

_____

_____

_____

_____